# BOOK SMART

## Also By Linda Griffin

Maximum Occupancy: How Smart Innkeepers Put Heads in Beds in Every Season

The Gratitude Book Project: Celebrating 365 Days of Gratitude (Anthology)

# BOOK SMART

**THE NINETY DAY GUIDE TO WRITING AND
SELF-PUBLISHING FOR BUSY ENTREPRE-
NEURS, BUSINESS OWNERS, AND CORPO-
RATE PROFESSIONALS**

## Linda Griffin

Velaris Books
ASHBURN, VIRGINIA

Linda Griffin/Velaris Books

22900 North Brown Sq.

Ashburn, Va. 20148

www.velarisbooks.com

Ordering Information:

Quantity Sales. Special discounts are available on quantity purchases by corporations, associations, and others. For details, contact the "Special Sales Department" at the address above.

Book Smart: The Ninety Day Guide to Writing and Self-Publishing
for Busy Entrepreneurs, Business Owners and Corporate Professionals / Linda Griffin. —1st ed.

ISBN 978-0-9829345-3-1

*To Mom and Dad*

# Contents

"It no longer matters how you publish, just that it gets published."

—The Future of Ink

# Preface

I was in a mild state of panic. I had just committed several thousand dollars to purchase booth space at the big International Innkeeping conference.

My plane ticket was purchased and the hotel room was reserved, adding another chunk of money to my total investment.

I planned to launch my first book at the conference. The book would be geared toward marketing for the bed and breakfast industry.

I was panicked because the conference was a little over three months away and the book didn't exist.

There's no better way to establish instant credibility than with a book and I didn't want to wait an entire year for the next conference.

I had a marketing process I used with clients and I wasn't a totally new writer having published a blog on a regular basis.

I knew I had to self-publish in order to meet my self-imposed deadline. There's no way I could acquire an agent, shop my book idea around, get a publishing contract, and complete the project in ninety days.

The traditional publishing process averages eighteen months to two years after the contract is signed.

I created my own crash course in self-publishing by purchasing books and doing extensive research on the internet. I learned all the bits and pieces that went into creating a quality book on a tight time line.

I wanted to produce a book quickly but I wasn't interested in just throwing something together. I wanted a book I could be proud to put my name on, one that would be equivalent in quality to a book published by one of the New York publishing houses.

I was able to get all the information I needed but I had to use multiple sources, including internet research, books on writing, and books on publishing.

The process wasn't pretty. I was literally checking the final proof of the book while working at another event.

The story does have a happy ending. I finished the book, *Maximum Occupancy*, just in time to have it shipped to the Innkeeping conference. Launching the book there helped me to successfully enter the bed and breakfast market and garnered new business for me.

A few months later, reflecting on everything I had learned, I knew there were other busy professionals who had a desire to write a book and build authority.

They don't have an interest in becoming a professional writer but they do want to share their knowledge, stand out from the competition and grow their business. I created a start to finish roadmap based on my experience to teach others how to write and self-publish a book that solves a problem.

My super power is the ability to build a path through a complex environment - a yellow brick road that can be followed step by step to get the desired results.

I turned my experience in self-publishing into a repeatable process which was the genesis of my book coaching program Fast Track to Author. This book contains my entire process. If you follow it, you can be a published author ninety days from today.

**This is the year you'll stop talking about writing a book and actually do it! My goal is to help you avoid the common self-publishing pitfalls and produce a well-written, beautifully designed book.**

I'm not going to ask you to lock yourself in a room, forsake your business commitments, your friends and your family, and not come out for ninety days.

What I'm asking you to do is to make writing your book a priority for the next ninety days. I'll give you lots of tips and tricks on how to get the writing done. Then I'll walk you through the book publishing process and book launch.

If the ninety-day schedule isn't right for you, but you'd still like to finish your book quickly, use the time line in this book as a guide and stretch it out to write your book in 180 days.

# Introduction

There's a popular statistic floating around that says eight out of ten people in the world want to write a book, however, only one in ten actually do.

Writing a book is hard work. It takes time and energy. It requires planning, research, and commitment to writing, publishing, and marketing. It's just too much for most people.

Why would a busy entrepreneur, business owner, or corporate professional take on the task of writing a book?

A book written by an expert is a business and career building tool. Writing a book will automatically position them head and shoulders above their competition.

Take inventory of your top three competitors, whether they're business owners or other professionals in your industry. How many of them have written a book?

When you're going head to head to win new business or get that promotion, which one of you will be more impressive? Of course, it's the person who wrote the book on your area of expertise.

A book positions you as an expert in your topic and raises your position to one of credible authority as opposed to salesperson.

*Book Smart* will guide you through the book writing and self-publishing process. It's organized into four sections which follow my Fast Track to Author Book Coaching Program:

- Section 1: Plan your book
- Section 2: Write your book
- Section 3: Publish your book
- Section 4: Launch your book

The program and the book are designed to take an author from idea to published in ninety days.

Throughout the book, you'll find Expert Author Action Steps that summarize the key learning points of the section. Here's the first one:

> **Expert Action Step:** Read the book all the way through before starting your book project. There are marketing steps which need to be taken in parallel with your writing activities in order to make your book launch successful.

Take notes and read the action steps to get an overview of the program. Once you understand the overall process, read through the book again, working through the action steps as you go.

**The Ninety Day Author Fast Track Schedule**

**Plan your book (Days 1 to 7)**

You'll decide on a topic, complete market research, determine your ideal reader, and define the problem you plan to help them solve. You'll create a mind map to get your ideas out of your head and create a framework for your writing.

**Write the first draft (Days 8 to 42)**

You'll start writing using a daily word count goal of between 600 and 900 words with total words in the first draft between 30,000 and 40,000. As you write the first draft, you'll build your writing muscles. You'll learn how to increase your productivity, stay motivated, break through stumbling blocks, and get re-energized if you hit the writing wall.

When you complete the first draft of your manuscript, you'll work on organizing the book into chapters and sections, choose the fonts you want to use in the finished book, finalize the title and subtitle, and create your author page on Amazon.

### Write the second draft (Days 43 to 56)

You'll send your manuscript to beta readers for feedback, check the flow of your book to ensure it matches your vision, and complete another round of self-editing.

### Prepare To Publish (Days 57 to 75)

In this step, you'll have fun working with a graphic designer to create your cover and send your manuscript to a professional editor for polishing. You'll use a book designer to format your manuscript for print.

## Publish, Print, and launch (Days 76 to 90)

You're at the finish line! In this step, you'll create a final print ready document and send it off to the printer. You'll set up a sales page on Amazon and/or your book web site, and launch your book.

Throughout the process, you'll complete marketing tasks to build buzz around your book leading to the launch date.

### Your Self-Publishing Team

Self-Publishing doesn't mean doing everything yourself. Many of the tasks leading up to the launch can be handled by a personal or virtual assistant. Other tasks, such as designing the book cover should be done by a professional.

I'll make recommendations of tasks to delegate in the appropriate chapters. Your Self-Publishing Team members could include:

**Author assistant**. You may already have a personal assistant or virtual assistant who can take on some of the administrative tasks of your book project. Depending on their skills, they can do things like sending your manuscript to an editor or scheduling your book launch.

**Professional editor**. You will be doing some self-editing as part of this program but the final edit needs to be done by someone who knows all the industry standard rules.

**Beta Readers**. Members of your target audience who will get an advance copy of your manuscript to provide feedback.

**Proofreader**. A professional who will provide the final quality assurance check before the book goes to the printer.

**Book interior designer**. You will use a writing app to create the manuscript. A book designer will take the content and lay out the pages in a pleasing style, with proper typesetting.

**Book cover designer**. The book cover is the first thing a potential reader will see. A book cover designer will combine colors, images, and type to ensure your book grabs attention.

**Book printer**. There are many options for getting your book printed, from print on demand services to a local print shop.

**Book Coach**. A book coach will provide structure to the project, guide you through writing and publishing, and help you avoid pitfalls.

The coach will recommend experts for the other team members you need such as editor and proofreader. Visit expertauthor411.com/work-with-me for a complete list of services I provide.

**Project costs**

One of the questions you probably have is how much it will cost to self-publish your book. The answer depends on how much you want to do yourself. I've provided a range below of what I consider reasonable costs. It will give you an idea for planning purposes.

 * ISBN – Free to $295

 * Book cover design - $30 - $250

 *Interior book design - $59 - $1600

 *Copy editing / proofing - $150 - $600

 *Printing costs per book - $4 -$7

*Linda Griffin*

12

# Part 1
# Plan Your Book

*"Whatever you can do or dream you can, begin it.*

*Boldness has genius, power, and magic in it."*

—Johann Wolfgang von Goethe

*Linda Griffin*

# CHAPTER 1

## The Ultimate Business Building Tool

There are many benefits to taking on the project of writing and publishing a book. Here are five compelling reasons you should consider writing a book this year:

### 1. Credibility

You probably face heavy competition in the marketplace, especially if you're a smaller company competing with a company with a larger staff or more resources.

When you can say you wrote the book in your area of expertise, you demonstrate your skill in a very tangible way and help to level the playing field.

### 2. Thought Leadership

Business owners and professionals hire coaches and consultants to help them break through stumbling blocks or achieve goals and objectives.

If they've had a previous bad experience that didn't produce the desired results, they may be jaded and skeptical of consultants who promised to help them take their business or career to the next level and didn't produce results.

A business coach/consultant who has documented their unique process in a book can use that book as part of their marketing efforts with a potential client. It will build trust and confidence in you and demonstrate your thought leadership.

### 3. Focus

Authoring a book can help a potential client identify where you can best help them immediately. Your large portfolio of services may be overwhelming to a potential client.

Writing a book that solves one problem will give you the opportunity to talk about one specific solution.

By starting with one problem, you get a quick win, increase the client's confidence in your abilities, and lead to more work.

## 4. Publicity

A book serves as the ultimate business card to attract new business. If you go to a Chamber of Commerce event and pass out a book rather than a business card, you will be remembered.

Having a book makes you a celebrity and gets you free publicity in the form of book reviews. It will open doors to speaking engagements at industry conferences, local groups, on television, radio, and podcasts.

How much do you spend on lead generation today? When you self-publish, you can print a book for five dollars or less. You have the potential to turn that five dollar investment into hundreds or thousands of dollars in new business.

## 5. Authority

Writing a book can help you launch into a new industry or business segment. When done correctly, writing a book makes you an authority in your book's topic.

If you're starting a business after a layoff, a book can fill the gap in your resume. Hiring managers will ask what you've been doing since you left your last company. It's impressive to respond with a discussion of your new book.

If you're between jobs, the process of writing a book can help you figure out what you want to do next.

When picking your book topic, you'll take an inventory of your skills and the problems you can help others solve. In the process, you might discover or re-discover skills you can add to your resume or use to exit the corporate world and start your own business.

# CHAPTER 2

## You're an Expert – Own It!

Every subject matter expert has the knowledge to write a book. You just need the right tools and the right process. If you've written blog posts, articles, or white papers, you already know how to write. I'll provide a structure to help you transfer your writing skills into a book format.

If you have no prior writing experience, you may need to hire a ghost writer or sign up for my personalized book coaching program where we outsource much of the process to an expert team.

The word expert can be intimidating. In fact, it's one of the reasons professionals don't write a book. They either feel everything has already been said about their topic or they feel their knowledge isn't deep enough to consider themselves an expert.

I agree with Corbett Barr of expertenough.com who says there are levels of expertise and you only need to be expert enough to help other people. On a scale of one to ten, your expertise may be at a six, which means you can help people who are at levels one through five.

When I needed a website for my business, I decided to build it myself using Wordpress. It's something I could have outsourced but it was fun for me because of my techie background. Over the years, I've built several sites for myself and for clients. I don't have the skills of a professional web designer who builds websites as their primary business but I have knowledge I can share with someone who wants to build a basic website using the Wordpress platform.

There's an almost unlimited amount of information on the web about Wordpress. If a person is too busy to search the web or doesn't feel confident in being able to pick out the best information, they might come to me for help as a subject matter expert.

As you embark on this journey to write and publish a book in ninety days, I encourage you to take stock of where your expertise lies on a continuum and identify people who are less experienced and could benefit from your help.

*Linda Griffin*

# CHAPTER 3

## Banish Long, Boring Books

Short is in style! I'm not just saying that because I'm only 5'3" tall. Readers want short books.

Just a few years ago, a book by an expert author was expected to be 400 pages long to ensure you were taken seriously. Books by experts in today's environment are around 150 to 200 pages. We'll validate that when you complete your market research on Amazon.

We live in a world of short attention spans and instant gratification. In an increasingly digital world, people's attention spans are short. In fact according to a study done by Microsoft, people lose concentration after only eight seconds!

Most people won't sit still long enough to read a 400 page book or they may feel intimidated by a book of that size. They want the sense of accomplishment that finishing a short book will give them. They want an expert to simplify the material into an easy to digest message or solution to their problem.

People who are used to watching videos on YouTube and surfing the web on their cell phones want visual content. They don't want to read page after page of single spaced, ten point type.

They're used to looking at web pages with lots of white space, photos, sub-headings, and lists. They want the same things in the books they're reading.

As writers, our goal is to produce a book that's going to be read and acted upon. Our books must give our readers the type of experience they've come to expect from other media.

We will give them what they want by providing less pages, larger type size, lists, headings, and checklists to put more white space on the page.

You'll be researching your topic as part of the next step in the planning process. I think you'll find the bestsellers in your category will all have something in common. They will be quick reads - under 200 pages. They will have short chapters and summaries of key points.

They will have stories, anecdotes, and case studies to illustrate major points. If you want your book to be well received, emulate those best sellers.

**Case Study:** My book *Maximum Occupancy: How Smart Innkeepers Put Heads in Beds in Every Season* is 144 pages long. It addresses a common problem that bed and breakfast owners have which is how to consistently fill their rooms.

Here's an excerpt from an Amazon review about the book: "I am the type that wishes authors would stop trying to impress people by writing two or three hundred pages and providing ten pages worth of content. This book has a reasonably high percentage of useful content. I do recommend it."

That quote illustrates exactly what I'm talking about.

Pick one specific problem or challenge that someone who isn't an expert would like to solve or overcome. Taking that approach will make it easier to create a well thought out book with high quality content.

Your finished book will likely be in the 130 page - 200 page range. It won't be possible to write everything you know about your subject in a book of that length. Think of this as your first book, not your only book.

We'll talk more about picking your topic in the Plan Your Book section.

# CHAPTER 4

## You Don't Need a Book Contract

Before the 1990s, the only way to publish a book was to get an agent, create a book proposal, and have the agent shop around for a buyer at one of the few large publishing houses.

You could bypass the traditional publishing route by using what was called a vanity publisher. They would publish your book but it would never be able to be sold in a bookstore or carried by a library.

New technology in book publishing as well as wide ranging distribution options have made self-publishing accessible to any aspiring author. For a busy professional, it means you can write and publish a book based on your expertise and use it to help you get more business without the constraints built into the traditional publishing model.

I knew self-publishing had arrived when I attended Book Expo America, the industry trade conference for publishing. I found many self-publishing vendors exhibiting on the show room floor and an entire educational track dedicated to self-publishing.

There's good news and bad news in this new development. Barriers to publishing have been removed but it's easy to produce an unprofessional book that doesn't follow the rules of good publishing. A book with an uninteresting cover, grammatical errors, and bad formatting screams 'self-published'.

At Book Expo, I attended a panel discussion with three A-List authors who discussed the pros and cons of traditional publishing vs. self-publishing.

## ADVANTAGES OF SELF-PUBLISHING

### 1. It takes less time and gives the author more control over the publishing process

The first reason to self-publish is time. The time line for traditional publishing is long. You must first acquire an agent by writing query letters. Your agent will then pitch your book to publishing houses to secure a book deal. If you're lucky enough to get a book deal, your book will be put on the publishing house schedule. It can take up to a year and a half or longer to actually get the book published.

## 2. Provides Rights Protection

When you sign with a publishing house, depending on the contract terms, the publishing house may own the rights to your work. If so, they will have the final decision on the cover design, the retail price, and where it's distributed.

## 3. Puts more money in your pocket

One of the attractions for publishing with one of the big publishing houses is receiving a monetary advance. For new authors who sign with a large publishing house, the advance is typically $10K - $15K. Smaller, independent publishing houses typically issue a $1K - $5K advance. As the name implies, an advance give the author money up front in anticipation of book sales. When the book goes on sale, author royalties are applied to the advance.

Only after the advance is fully covered do the royalties come to the author. With author royalties averaging fifteen to twenty-five percent of the sales price, the advance check is the biggest one they will ever see. In some cases, it's the only check they see.

As a self-published author, your royalty will be between thirty-five percent and one hundred percent depending on how you distribute your book. With no advance to worry about, you start making money day one.

## 4. Extends Marketing Control

Traditional publishers will handle the logistics of getting your book into bookstores but they provide minimal publicity and marketing. The author is expected to do that on their own. These days, a publishing house rarely takes on a brand new author. The author needs to already have a following and a proven track record to reduce the risk of investing in them.

In the time it takes you to craft a book proposal, send it out, and wait for responses, you could have a self-published book in your hand with pre-sales already committed. Your author platform could be up and running, connecting you with potential readers and future clients.

If your book is successful, you may find one of the big publishing houses knocking on your door and offering to produce your next book!

*Linda Griffin*

# CHAPTER 5

## Shake off Self- Sabotage

As a busy leader, you're confident, driven, and have already achieved success in one or more areas. Becoming an author will require learning a new set of skills.

Completing your book project might bring up some negative self- talk. I view this as gremlins lurking in the shadows to shake your confidence. I want to expose the four most common gremlins for new writers and give you some strategies to make them disappear.

### Writing Gremlin #1 –

### You can always write the book later

You already have a lot of demands on your time. When you're under pressure, gremlin number one will whisper in your ear that you can put your book project on the back burner.

I have personal experience with this gremlin. When I lived in New Jersey, my home was about a 45-minute drive from New York City. You would think living so close to the big city, I would take the opportunity to go in as often as I could to take advantage of the shopping and entertainment.

In reality, I lived there for over 10 years, but I can count the number of times I actually went into the city. Why was that? I knew I could go at any time, consequently, I never went. I thought I had all the time in the world. The few times I visited New York City were when I was entertaining out of town guests. Fast forward, ten years later and I took a new job assignment in Virginia. All of a sudden, time ran out.

Gremlin #1 whispers we'll always have time to finish our book later.

Fight this gremlin by thinking about the people who would benefit from reading your book right now. You owe it to them and to yourself to finish it as soon as possible. Act as if it's now or never and get your book written so you can attract more clients, raise your authority level, and help more people.

## Writing Gremlin #2 –

## I have too many other demands on my time

Meet the brother to Gremlin #1. He's a whiner. His mantra is "If only". If only you could lock yourself away or go to a desert island to write. If only the family didn't need so much attention. If only the job or business wasn't so demanding.

Gremlin #2 wants you to be a victim of circumstance. He wants you to believe someone else or something else has to change before you can get what you want.

Knock out Gremlin #2 by changing your reaction to things you can't control.

You have 24 hours in a day. Your kids, your spouse, and your business commitments can take up all of those hours if you let them. Make your book a priority. Commit to yourself you will make the time to write. If it means getting up earlier, staying up later, or carving out a block of time in the middle of the day, you will do whatever it takes to make your book a reality.

## Writing Gremlin #3 – I don't know enough

Gremlin #3 tries to undermine your self-confidence by telling you there are many other people more qualified than you to write on your topic. This gremlin was at work when it never occurred to me during my corporate career to write white papers and articles for industry journals. I had expert training and job experience but I didn't consider myself at the same level as one of my colleagues who built authority and industry credibility by writing articles.

Eliminate this gremlin by recognizing that expertise in any subject resembles a continuum more than a discrete point. You might be at a level 3 or level 4 in a particular skill, but there are lots of people at a level 1 or a level 2. You're already an expert to those people!

## Writing Gremlin #4 – I might fail

The last writing gremlin plays on your pride. I'm sure you're already successful in your business or career. You're already a high performer and probably a perfectionist. You don't want to look foolish by publishing a book that doesn't meet your personal standards.

Defeat Gremlin #4 by reading and applying what you learn in this book. It provides all the resources you'll need to write and publish a book you can be proud to put beside a big New York publishing house book.

*Linda Griffin*

# CHAPTER 6

## Determine Your 'Why'

When I was writing *Maximum Occupancy*, a friend of mine told me there was no reason for me to jump on the bandwagon and write a book.

My friend said there are plenty of successful business coaches and consultants who haven't written a book. In their experience, those who did write a book didn't make a lot of money.

All of that is true. The average business book sells fewer than two hundred copies over the life of the book.

My reasons for writing a book weren't to become a NY Times bestseller. I wanted to establish credibility in the Bed and Breakfast industry. I wanted to use the book as lead generation to attract clients.

I wanted to re-purpose the content into paid classes and use the book as the basis for paid speaking engagements. I was able to accomplish all those goals with *Maximum Occupancy*.

I like to compare writing a book to winning a gold medal at the Olympics. A medal gives the owner instant credibility as an elite athlete and sets them apart from every other athlete in the same sport.

Some winners use that celebrity, credibility and authority to build a coaching business. Others build speaking businesses. Regardless of what the athlete does after winning the medal, their name will always be linked with the Olympic champion title.

After you become a published author, your name will always be linked with the credibility and authority of being an expert in your industry.

---

**Expert Author Action Step: Write down your 'Why'.**
**Here are some examples:**

- Build credibility as an industry expert

- Be more competitive for opportunities

- Use the book as a calling card with potential clients

- Make money selling books

- Get speaking engagements and industry interviews

- Create paid online courses based on the book

- Start or grow a consulting business

- Conduct live workshops based on the book

- Create multiple streams of income by selling products and services related to your book

---

*Linda Griffin*

# CHAPTER 7

## When an eBook Just Isn't Enough

Some authors decide to produce an eBook as opposed to going to the additional expense of producing a printed book.

I have an eReader and I love it. Before eBooks, whenever I went on vacation, I had to reserve a certain amount of suitcase space for books, and I always worried I wouldn't take enough to last me through the entire vacation.

Now, I can download as many books as I want in advance and have plenty of reading material.

eBooks have changed the publishing landscape dramatically. The popularity of eBooks has caused some to predict the end of printed books. As an avid reader, I disagree.

I purchase some printed books by favorite authors because I want to have a complete set of their writing. Other purchases may be special editions that I want to keep as collectibles.

The most common reason I purchase a physical book is when I plan to use it for research or reference.

Although most eReaders allow you to make notes and highlight passages, I find it cumbersome to do that electronically. I like to put sticky notes on key pages, underline important points, and make notes in the margins.

Print books are an imperative component of your overall marketing plan. When you finish writing your manuscript, you've already done the hardest part of the project.

A print book will leverage your intellectual capital to its maximum potential to build authority and credibility. Here are eight places where having an eBook just isn't enough:

**At your book launch**

Book launches aren't just for famous authors. I recommend scheduling a book launch as an accountability task.

The act of putting an event on the calendar and notifying your friends and family puts you on the hook to finish your book on time. It can be as simple as hosting a wine and cheese event at your home or as elaborate as renting a formal event venue.

Your friends and family are going to want a signed copy of your book and you're going to want to document the event with photos of them holding your book.

## At Conferences and Trade shows

I launched my first book at an industry conference. Although I grossly over estimated the number of copies I would sell, I had physical copies that people could thumb through and purchase on the spot.

Having a stack of books on my table attracted passers-by who were intrigued by the cover.

Whenever I speak at a conference, I always request permission to sell my book in the back of the room or host a book signing at a vendor table during the event.

After hearing you speak or conduct a workshop, attendees are likely to want to connect with you further by purchasing your book.

## At local events

I volunteer with a non-profit organization and earlier this year, I chaired a committee that hosted an author showcase event for the community. Each author was given a table to sell their books.

One of the authors didn't have any physical books. All of his books were digital. As you can imagine, his table looked very sparse with only a stack of postcards next to all of the other authors who had books displayed.

## In the trunk of your car

You heard me correctly. Always keep a few copies of your book in your car.

There have been several times when I've met people in informal situations, and in the conversation, I've mentioned my book.

I was pleasantly surprised the first time someone asked if I had a copy with me and whether they could purchase it.

They make a wonderful impression when you gift one to a potential client or business partner. I never leave home without a few books in the trunk.

## For contest entries

Entering a contest or getting a review from a publication are excellent ways to get publicity for your book and your business. Some of them require that you send a physical copy.

## On your web site and social media accounts

You can post a cover of your eBook on your website and on your social media accounts, but you can't post a picture of yourself or your fan holding a copy of the book. Posting photos of fans holding your book is a form of social proof. It lets potential book buyers know that other people like your book and it may entice them to make a purchase.

## To get media reviews

You're going to be reaching out to various media sources such as reporters and magazines inviting them to review your book. While many of them will accept a pdf version, some will want a hard copy.

There are times when you'll want to send a hard copy to an important reviewer. An email with an attachment can get lost but it's hard to ignore a physical book delivered to their desk.

**For giveaways and publicity**

Chamber of commerce events, networking events, and functions hosted by local business organizations are perfect opportunities to donate a copy of your book as a door prize or give-away.

Usually at these events, the donors are recognized and in some cases, are allowed to address the group. This gives you an opportunity to showcase not only your book, but your business as well.

Bottom line: Don't choose between an eBook and a printed book. Produce both versions!

# CHAPTER 8

## Define the Book's Audience

I recommend your finished book be under two hundred pages. It will automatically narrow the book's focus to one specific area of your expertise.

After you narrow the focus, the next step is to figure out who will benefit the most from reading the finished book. Understanding who that person is will set the tone for your writing.

I had a client whose topic dealt with an innovative program to ensure young African American boys finished high school and went on to college. The tone and substance of her book would differ depending on whether she was writing it for parents, teachers, or the school system.

We discussed how the format of the book would support the goals of her consulting business. Two of the format options were a step by step guide to implementing the program or a case study of the successful pilot

49

program. Different types of readers will be attracted to the book depending on its format.

**To narrow your book topic and define the audience:**

1. Make a list of problems someone could encounter in your area of expertise.

2. Beside each problem, identify the specific person or group of people who are looking for a solution to that problem.

3. For each problem, describe a solution you could provide in book format.

**Example:**

**Area of expertise:** Travel Consultant

**Problem:** Fear of traveling alone

**Audience:** Women business travelers

**Solution:** Tips on how to travel safely in the U.S. and abroad

You'll notice in this example, we chose women business travelers. Had we chosen women traveling for fun, or recent college graduates traveling alone for the first time, the tone and focus of the book would be different.

Taking the time up front to think about the problem, solution, and audience for your book will make writing the first draft of your manuscript easier and faster.

Don't put yourself into the almost impossible position of trying to find a unique problem no one else has ever written a book about.

It may be counter intuitive but you should be doing the exact opposite. If a book hasn't been written on your topic, it's probably because there's no market for it.

The better approach is to find a topic that has been done before and put your unique spin on it.

For example, there are hundreds of books written on the topic of leadership. Your expertise might be working with entry level managers.

You could write a book about the leadership qualities needed to succeed in a first time management job. Of course, you'll find other books aimed at first time managers, but your personal stories, case studies, or your special process will make the book unique.

You're writing a book to ultimately build your business. Decide even before you start writing how the book will fit into your marketing and sales strategy.

Think about the steps you want the reader to take after reading the book. That way you can put breadcrumbs throughout the book that lead the reader to the logical next step or you can put a call to action in the back of the book to give them direction.

---

**Expert Author Action Step:** Write a description of your ideal reader, the problem you can help them solve, and your solution.

Don't worry if you're considering more than one problem/solution at this point. You'll narrow it down in the next chapter with topic research.

---

# CHAPTER 9

## Will it Sell?

After you've narrowed the topic for your book, the next step in the writing process is to research other books in your area of expertise.

You want to find out whether other books on your topic are selling. You don't want to write about a topic that has no competition. If other authors are publishing books about your topic, it means the topic has already proven itself to be marketable.

By studying other books in the market, you can get an idea of whether your book will sell.

There are several sources you can use to complete market research.

Start with your personal library. As you were building expertise in your chosen topic area, I'm sure you purchased books as part of the learning process.

Other sources for market research are the local library or bookstore.

My favorite way to do market research for books is to use Amazon. Not only can you complete the research at your convenience, day or night, but Amazon gives you access to book sales information you won't get from your library or book store.

Amazon is one of the largest search engines in the world and they keep lots of statistics that will help you position your book.

I recently completed research for a client's book project. She was writing a book about using your personal style to reflect your business brand.

To start the research, I entered the keywords 'beauty', 'style', and 'grooming' one at a time and analyzed the results. I looked for best sellers in those categories.

If the results didn't seem pertinent or if there were no recently published books, I switched to related keywords. I also noted the books that showed up in the 'customers also bought' section.

When I found several books similar to the one my client wanted to write, I created a spreadsheet with:

- The title of each book
- The format (hardcover or paperback)
- The problem the book proposed to solve
- The number of pages in the book
- The retail price
- The book dimensions
- The year it was published
- The Amazon categories

You can follow the same process to research your book topic.

As you research, use the 'look inside' feature of Amazon. It gives you the first ten percent of the book which usually includes the table of contents and a portion of the first chapter.

Look for ways you could bring a unique perspective to the topic based on your experience. Could you improve upon the topic by providing a different point of view or filling in gaps the book doesn't cover? Is there a segment of readers who've been overlooked?

Next, read the book reviews. In particular, read the three star reviews. Those reviewers liked the book but felt there was something missing. You might be able to address their concerns in your book.

In these early stages of your book project, you're using the research to hone in on your topic prior to completing your mind map.

Later on, you'll use the research to help position your book's retail price and find potential book reviewers.

Finally, make note of the cover design of each book. For my research, I did a screen shot of each cover and provided that to my client. We used the screen shots later on in the project when we were discussing the cover elements for her book.

After completing the research, you'll be confident your topic is marketable and you'll have a good idea of the other books competing for buyers in the space.

---

**Author Fast Track Action Step: Finalize your book topic**

---

# CHAPTER 10

## Don't Outline – Mind Map Instead

You've narrowed down your topic and identified your ideal reader. It's time to start mapping out your book.

Traditionally, writers create an outline but I've found an outline can be restrictive. It forces you to write in a linear fashion which isn't always the most productive way to write. Instead, I like to use a mind map for book outlining.

A mind map will:

- Get all of the important ideas about your topic written down
- Identify areas that will later become chapters, subheadings, table of contents items, or paragraphs in the finished book
- Uncover areas where more research is needed
- Help you avoid writer's block

Mind map tools run the gamut from low tech to high tech. You can use any one of them based on your personal preference.

The simplest and most low tech way to mind map is to simply draw it on a piece of paper.

**Here's how to mind map on paper:**

1. Write the main topic of your book down in the center of a piece of paper and draw a circle around it

2. Below the circle, write one concept you want to share in the finished book. Make it a short phrase, four or five words. Circle it and connect the two circles. Circle number two becomes a sub-topic.

3. If you have a new idea related to circle number two, write it down and connect it to circle two.

4. Keep writing concepts and connecting them to the appropriate circle until you have all of your ideas down on paper.

Another way to mind map is by using index cards. On each card, write down one major concept. Write subtopics connected to the concept on the card. After you have all of the ideas written on cards, you can shuffle and organize them into the flow you want your book to take.

The drawback to either of the pen and paper options is that you'll have to manually transfer the mind map into your writing application and it won't be easy to move topics around or make changes without rewriting the paper mind map.

I like to use a mind mapping app to give me more flexibility and increased productivity. My personal preference is the writing app, Scrivener (MAC and Windows).

It's my recommendation for mind mapping, writing, and compiling the manuscript for publication.

Scrivener was developed specifically for writers and is filled with features to help write, format, and compile your book for printing. Throughout the rest of this book, I'll refer to Scrivener as we move to the topics of writing, editing, and printing your finished manuscript. Visit expertauthor411.com/resources for a link to the Scrivener free trial along with links to other tools I use.

Scrivener has a cork board view which is perfect for mind mapping. I simply create cards for each of my major mind map topics.

Sub-topics can be created underneath each main card like paper index cards. I end up with a card stack with the main topic on top and the subtopics underneath.

If I decide to move a topic or sub-topic, I simply drag the card to the new position. When I start writing, I can drag each text block to re-order sections, chapters, or blocks of text.

Your mind map will be a work in progress for the first few weeks of writing. As you write, you may find that you've left some things out or certain sub-topics really belong under a different major topic. If that happens, go back to the mind map and modify as needed.

**A few words about Microsoft Word:** If you decide to use Microsoft Word as your writing app, I recommend you write each of your major mind map topics on a separate page or in a separate Word document.

This will give you the flexibility to move topics around and re-order them.

Use the Word commands and tools to format. It will save you headaches when you create the final print ready file.

| |
|---|
| **Expert Author Action Step:** Mind Map your topic |

*Linda Griffin*

# CHAPTER 11

## Your Book Structure and Framework

The last step in planning your book is to pick the structure of your book. Take a look at your mind map and study the concepts and topics you want to include.

What format would give your readers the best chance of absorbing your knowledge and taking action? Some of the most common formats for non-fiction books are:

- **Tip Book:** A compilation of tips on a particular subject. Example: 50 ways to save money on your taxes.

- **List Book:** Similar to a Tip Book. It may be in the format of a checklist. Example: 100 free or almost free decorations for your wedding

- **Prescription Book:** Gives the reader a game plan or path to solve a specific problem. Example: The total home office makeover

- **Anthology Book:** Takes a specific topic and invites multiple authors to write a chapter. Example: Any of the Chicken Soup for the Soul series

- **One Big Idea Book:** Focuses and expounds upon one big idea. Example: The Tipping Point

- **Question and Answer Book:** One topic, written in a question and answer format. Example: Forty Questions about interpreting the Bible

- **Memoir or Biography Book:** a historical account or biography written from personal knowledge. Example: The Glass Castle: A Memoir

While the bulk of your book's content will fit into one of the formats above, you'll probably include aspects of the other formulas.

For example, my book *Maximum Occupancy* is a prescription book which solves the problem of getting a consistent flow of reservations for a Bed and Breakfast Innkeeping business.

In the book, I include lists, questions and answers, and anecdotes about my personal life.

**Author Fast Track Action Step: Pick the structure for your book**

*Linda Griffin*

# Part 2

# Write Your Book

"Whatever the mind of man can conceive and believe, it can achieve."

— Napoleon Hill

*Linda Griffin*

# CHAPTER 12

## Get in the Writing Zone

I had an idea to write a book for quite a while but the idea didn't come to fruition until much later. I attended a speaker's conference in 2008 to learn how to incorporate paid speaking engagements into my business.

During one of the breaks, I went up on stage, held a microphone in one hand and a book in the other and visualized myself holding my own book and speaking on stage.

That was a great start but I didn't follow through on the idea with an action plan. Consequently, my dream of becoming a published author remained a dream.

I didn't make the commitment until 2012 when I actually moved beyond the idea, created a plan and made my book a reality.

Part of my problem was a self-limiting belief that I wasn't a writer. I was a math major in college and after graduation, I had a successful career at a Fortune 500 technology company. I thought of myself as a bits and bytes person, not a words person.

By 2008, even though I was successfully writing a blog on a regular basis, in my mind, I thought writing a book was beyond my capability. All the books I'd seen that were based on someone's expert knowledge were 300-400 pages long.

You may not have the same self-limiting belief I did, but something has been holding you back from completing your book. Before we start the writing process, there are three things I want you to do to mentally prepare:

## 1. Have an abundance mindset

Believe that all the resources you'll need to complete your book will be made available to you once you fully commit yourself to the project.

There are a lot of steps in the process of writing a book. There's the time it takes to write it, proofreading, editing, creating a cover, finding a printer, and launching the book to name a few.

Know that if you make the time to do the writing, all of the other pieces of the puzzle will come together and you will realize your dream.

## 2.    Set the intention

You may feel the timing isn't perfect for writing a book. Maybe you're getting ready for a big project at work or have family obligations coming up.

There is never an optimum time to start a book project. There's only your commitment to make it happen and your intention that nothing is going to stop you.

The best way I know of to set the intention is to create an accountability event. My accountability event was the industry conference where I launched my book. It gave me a hard deadline and a sense of urgency to complete the project.

If you don't have an industry event, use a local event, a speaking engagement, or a launch party you will host. Pick a date, make a deposit on the venue, and announce it to family, friends, and co-workers.

## 3.    Visualize success

One of the tricks elite athletes use is to picture themselves winning. They imagine the sights, smells and sounds of the entire competition.

They go through the motions they'll perform on the ski slope or the diving board.

When you watch an ice skating competition on TV and they cut to a scene of the athletes waiting backstage for their turn, you'll see many of them twirling, gliding, and jumping even though they don't have skates on.

They're visualizing successfully completing their routine. Picture yourself at a book signing or standing on stage holding your book.

Napoleon Hill, author of the classic book, *Think and Grow Rich* says thoughts are things. Whatever you think will happen, your subconscious mind will bring to fruition.

Let's start writing the first draft of your book!

# CHAPTER 13

## Put Pen to Paper

You need six things to successfully complete the first draft of your manuscript:

1. A topic that includes your target audience, their problem, and your solution
2. A decision on the book structure (tips, prescription, memoir, etc.)
3. A mind map (What I use instead of a traditional book outline)
4. A writing tool (Microsoft Word is good but Scrivener is better)
5. A writing plan that meets the publish date
6. A writing ritual that includes the frequency, timing and word count

Let's take these one at a time.

**A topic that attracts your target audience, a description of their problem, and your solution**

Refer to the topic research you completed.

**Your ideal reader**

Picture having a conversation with one of your ideal readers and write as if you're speaking with them in person.

The ideal reader is the person who's going to read your book, really love your book, and recommend it to others.

Of course, someone who's not your ideal reader can always purchase your book. If you write a book for women business owners but a male business owner purchases it, that's perfectly fine.

The idea is to maximize the attraction your book will have to your ideal reader in order to maximize sales.

From a marketing perspective, the more you write to a specific audience, the easier it will be to attract them to your book.

**Describe your ideal reader's problem**

You want to be crystal clear on the problem your book will solve. Your readers don't care about the amount of effort you've put into writing the book. They care about their problem and getting a solution to that problem.

Your solution might be inspirational, practical, or aspirational. Decide exactly what you're going to be giving them.

A friend of mine, Cheree Warrick, wrote a book titled *Creating Business Plans that Actually Get Financed: How successful entrepreneurs and inventors position their companies to receive financing from banks, Angel Investors, and venture capitalists.*

Her ideal reader is mentioned in the subtitle of the book: entrepreneurs and inventors. When someone reads the title, they know if the book was written for them before buying it.

**The book's structure**

Verify the book structure you picked when planning the project. Here's a recap:

- Tip Book: A compilation of tips on a particular subject. Example: 50 ways to save money on your tax return.

- List Book: Similar to a Tip Book. It may be in the format of a checklist. Example: 100 free or almost free decorations for your wedding
- Prescription Book: Gives the reader a game plan or path to solve a specific problem. Example: The total home office makeover
- Anthology Book: Takes a specific topic and invites multiple authors to write a chapter. Example: Any of the Chicken Soup for the Soul series
- One Big Idea Book: Focuses and expounds upon one big idea. Example: The Tipping Point
- Question and Answer Book: One topic, written in a question and answer format. Example: Forty Questions about interpreting the Bible
- Memoir or Biography Book: a historical account or biography written from personal knowledge. Example: The Glass Castle: A Memoir

**A Mind Map**

In each writing session, you'll pick a topic or concept from your mind map and start writing the content. As you write, you may discover topics you want to add, delete, or change in the mind map.

If you think a topic no longer fits in the finished book, don't delete it from the mind map. Leave it in the mind map as a placeholder in case you want to add it to a different section of the book.

In Scrivener, I drag those topics to the bottom of the manuscript to move them out of the main flow.

Don't be concerned about writing in sequencing initially. With self-contained topics in your mind map, it's easy to pick one to write about in your daily writing session. Later, you'll combine these topics into chapters and sections.

## A Writing Tool

I recommend Scrivener as the writing tool because of its flexibility and functions designed for writers.

If you use Scrivener, select the nonfiction manuscript template. If you use Microsoft Word, put each mind map topic on a separate page or in a separate document to be combined later.

Refresh yourself on the elements of writing style. Nothing screams amateur self-publisher like writing that doesn't use correct grammar or sentence structure.

When you send your book for professional line editing and proofreading, they will catch errors, but you want to have as clean a manuscript as possible before you send it to editing.

**A Writing Plan**

Writing a book is like running a marathon. A first time marathoner doesn't get up on race day and decide to run 26.2 miles. They create a training plan and execute it in the weeks leading up the race.

The number of minutes it takes them to run a mile will vary based on their energy level, what they ate, or how much sleep they got the night before.

In each training session, they track the length of time they run and the number of miles they complete to calculate their pace. Over time, they learn how to increase the pace and predict how long it will take them to finish the marathon.

You're going to use their technique and apply it to your writing. You'll write every day, track the words you write in each writing session, and learn to pace yourself to get your manuscript finished in time to meet the book launch date.

If you were working with a traditional publisher, you would have a due date to finish the first draft. When you self-publish, you don't have an outside person to hold you accountable.

One of my tasks as a book coach is to act as an accountability partner for my clients. If you're going it alone, as I recommended in an earlier chapter, create an artificial deadline by announcing a launch date to your circle of contacts, friends, and family.

When you announce a launch date and schedule a book launch event, you create a deadline and a sense of urgency.

## Daily Writing Goal - Between 600 and 900 words

As discussed earlier, I expect your book to be 130 pages to 200 pages in length depending on the type of book you write.

A prescription book will have more pages than a tips book due to the nature of the information being shared. The length of an anthology book will depend on the number of contributors and the length of their chapters.

A good rule of thumb is to plan for the first draft of your manuscript to be around 33,000 to 40,000 words. After you write for a while, you can adjust the plan as the manuscript unfolds.

If this is your first book, 33,000 words may seem daunting but keep in mind 600 words is only three to four paragraphs in each writing session.

When I started blogging, it would take two hours to write a 500-word blog post. After developing my writing muscle, I can now write and edit a 500-word blog post in only 45 minutes.

The more you write, the easier it is to get into a groove and write 600 high quality words quickly.

**A Writing Ritual**

To make it easier to complete the daily word count goal, create a ritual. Developing a writing habit is just like learning any other habit. You have to do it on a regular basis and you have to set yourself up for success.

Make a daily appointment with yourself for the time of day and length of time you plan to write.

Put it on your calendar as a meeting and keep it religiously just as if it were a business meeting. Pick the time of day based on your personal situation and your energy level.

I like to write first thing in the morning and complete my word quota before the phone starts ringing. I've found my energy level and creativity is stronger early in the day.

I ensure it gets done by making writing my top priority and first project work of the day.

You may prefer to write on your lunch break, or in the evening after dinner. At the start of your writing appointment, go to your ideal writing location, and remove all distractions.

It might be a closed room away from family or with headphones on if you like to listen to music while you're working. Put the cell phone away or set it to vibrate. Close the email and social media windows on your computer.

In the first few writing sessions, write at your own pace and don't worry about the word count. You'll begin to write faster as you build your writing muscle.

Count the number of words you write in each session and record on a tracking sheet. You can download a free tracking sheet at

www.expertauthor411.com/booksmart.

Tracking your writing sessions will help you answer these questions:

- What is the best time of day for me to write?
- When is my energy and concentration level at its highest?
- When am I less likely to be interrupted?
- How quickly do I write?

**Determine your average daily word count**

Let's assume you write for an hour a day for five days. By counting the number of words you write in each session and calculating the average, you'll come up with an average daily word count. Now you know your writing pace.

You can use it to estimate how long it will take you to complete the first draft. If you write 600 words per day, you will finish the first draft in 55 days.

Don't expect to write very quickly at first. You're not yet in the writing zone. As you continue to write each day, your pace will naturally increase. You'll start to write faster and more accurately.

By the time your book is finished, you'll find you're writing more words per hour than you ever thought you would!

In Scrivener, you'll see the word count at the bottom of the edit window. Let's say you've decided to write for an hour, check the word count to see how many words you wrote.

If you didn't write 600 words, you know you'll need to add another writing session. Over time, you'll learn how to pace your writing to meet the word quota.

I want you to write every day. Try not to write Monday through Friday and take the weekend off because you'll lose momentum. After taking two days off, when Monday rolls around, your brain has to reset. You're not in the writing zone anymore.

If writing on certain days is really hard, consider cutting back the time. Write for fifteen minutes instead of thirty. You may find that the opposite is true. You're able to write fifteen minute a day during the week but an hour a day on the weekend.

That's okay. As long as you write something every day, you're building a habit. Share your schedule with the family. Let them know your writing schedule.

One of the worst things for a writer is to have a blank page and wonder what you're supposed to be writing next. When you have a mind map, you always have a topic you can write about.

Don't worry about sequencing and writing in order. Suppose you're working on a particular section of the book and plan to include an interview but the interview hasn't happened.

If you were writing sequentially, you would have to stop and wait until the interview was complete.

When you're writing out of sequence, you can move on to a different part of the book, work on it, and come back to the previous section after you've done the interview.

Don't write and edit at the same time. We're used to getting something right the first time and the tendency is to correct errors as we see them.

If you edit while writing, your productivity will suffer. Don't bother about spell check. Don't bother about run on sentences. Don't even bother trying to make paragraphs unless it comes naturally to you.

Just keep writing to get all of the information out of your head and into your manuscript. That's how you get the book done. Clean-up and sequencing comes later.

Scrivener can help you keep the momentum going. It has the ability to mark inline annotations and footnotes. For example, suppose you want to include a quote by Mark Twain in the section you're writing but you don't remember the exact quote.

You can put an annotation in your document to remind yourself to add the quote. Make annotated notes to yourself in color so you can easily see if there are things you need to look up or information you want to verify.

Finally, don't overdo it. Don't try to write for three hours and exhaust yourself. Start with fifteen or thirty minutes and work up to thirty minutes or an hour.

Two hours is probably the maximum you want to write at one sitting to prevent burnout. You could build in a short break during your writing time as well. Write for 15 minutes, take a two minute break, and get back to it.

---

**Expert Author Action Steps:**

1. Purchase Scrivener

2. Transfer your mind map into Scrivener

3. Start writing content from your mind map sections

4. Create a writing ritual. Try out different times of day and different durations to see what is most productive for you.

5. Calculate your average daily word count

---

# CHAPTER 14

## Techniques to Get Back on Track after Losing Momentum

One problem every runner faces is called hitting the wall. It happens when they use up the initial burst of energy they had at the start of the race.

When the race kicks off, they feel well prepared. They're fired up and energetic. They're cruising along at the desired pace.

At some point in the race, the runner has used up the quick energy they got from carb-loading the night before and the body starts getting tired.

Recognizing the fatigue, the brain starts sending more blood to the muscles. Unfortunately, that depletes the blood reserve in the brain so it starts to lose focus.

The brain is thinking, "Wait a minute, what are we doing here? What are you trying to make the body do? I don't remember agreeing to go 26.2 miles!" Next the brain and the muscles band together and try to convince the runner to lay down in the street and give up.

The best runners anticipate hitting the wall and plan for it. They have strategies and techniques that will help them get past the mental and physical block.

Writers need plans and strategies to help us get past writing blocks. Our finish line is getting our completed book in hand.

At the beginning of a book project, you're excited about writing a book and getting it published. It's been your dream for a long time.

You start out with high energy, writing every day, and meeting the daily word count target. Then life intrudes.

Maybe you get sick and can't write for a few days. Perhaps a family situation pops up that takes your attention away from writing.

Maybe you realize this writing thing is harder than you thought and you've got a lot more words to write to finish your manuscript on schedule.

Whatever the reason, you find yourself thinking, "Am I ever going to finish this book?"

When I wrote *Maximum Occupancy*, I hit the writing wall when I started to self-edit the first draft. After letting the book sit for several days, I picked it up and started to read it out loud. I was in shock! I didn't like the flow of the book at all.

I removed huge chunks of writing and reordered some sections of the book. There were several days when I thought I was never going to finish in time to get the book to the conference.

In fact, I was still re-writing when the book should have already gone to a professional editor.

If you're having problems meeting your writing goals or are getting discouraged, try taking one or more of the temporary actions below to get back on track. Then go back to your original writing schedule.

1. Remind yourself of your 'Why'
2. Review and adjust the days and times you've scheduled to write
3. Increase the time of each writing session

4.    Temporarily increase your target daily word count

5.    Change your writing ritual

6.    Add more accountability

Let's take them one at a time:

**Remind yourself of your 'Why'.**

You're writing a book to help other people solve a problem. Those people need your help. You owe it to your audience, your target reader to get your book out in the world so you can help them.

One of my Author Fast Track students was writing a book to show families how to recover after the loss of a matriarch or patriarch.

She had gotten off schedule and we were discussing options to get back on track. Reflecting on her 'why' really helped.

She had heard of two families who were dealing with the exact situation covered in her book. Those families would have benefited had they been able to purchase the book.

## Review and adjust the days and times you've scheduled to write

Maybe other commitments have prevented you from writing on the days you had scheduled. If so, consider adding a few more writing sessions to your week until you catch up.

## Increase the time of each writing session

If you originally scheduled 30 minutes a day, increase the time to one hour a day or schedule a second 30 minute writing session. It would theoretically double the number of words you could complete.

Be careful you don't over extend yourself with this option. I know I can only write about two hours a day in one session before I get tired and lose focus.

If you have another 10,000 words to write, don't try to do it in one weekend. Winners learn how to adjust and keep going to get to the finish line.

Runners celebrate finishing a race even if they had to run at a slower pace or crawl across the finish line. The same thing holds true for you. Whether you meet the original publication date or not, don't give up and you will celebrate with a published book!

**Temporarily increase your target daily word count.**

Check the average daily word count up to this point. Pull out the word tracking tool and track your word count for a week to see how much you get done in each writing session.

In running, there's a term called a negative split. In a negative split, you run the second half of the race faster than you ran the first half.

When applied to writing, you write the second half of the book faster by increasing your daily word count. Estimate how many more words you'll need to write to complete your first draft and try to pick up the pace.

**Change your writing ritual**

Look at your writing ritual - the time of day, the location, and the length of time you write - and tweak that.

Don't fight your natural energy levels. If writing in the early morning isn't working, try writing at lunch time or in the evening.

If writing at home has been too distracting, try going to the library or a coffee shop. Whatever the ideal writing situation is for you, try to make it happen on a more consistent basis.

## Add more accountability

If your book project has moved to the bottom of your To Do list, here are some ways to add accountability:

**Schedule your book launch event.** It doesn't have to be a big event but it needs to be one that gives you a sense of urgency and embarrassment if you don't meet the commitment. Send friends and family a formal invitation or save the date card for your book launch and announce it on social media.

**Pick an accountability partner.** Tell them you will check in with them daily via email, phone call, or text and report the number of words you've written.

**Send one or two sample chapters** to people on your mailing list and let them know you're part way through the book. Tell them when it's going to be finished and let them know you're going to be looking for beta readers when the manuscript is finished.

**Make a bet with yourself.** One of my mentors gave me this tip. If you don't finish the book by your target date, you will have to make a monetary contribution to a political campaign where you don't like the candidate. That's a pretty strong incentive!

### Finally, Be Realistic.

Let's say you've been averaging 300 words per day instead of 600. You've tried some of the strategies above and you just can't increase your pace. Adjust your schedule and target date. Let's go back to our marathon runner. Their primary goal is to finish the race. I'm not a marathon runner but I approach my projects with the same goal – to finish. There are thousands of people who have a book in their head and will never get it published.

Whether you finish your book in another six weeks or in another six months, you're still way ahead of all those other people who wish they could say they're a published author.

If you've tried all of the techniques above and need more help, contact me for assistance. We can discuss other options such as ghost writing.

*Linda Griffin*

# CHAPTER 15

## Create a Logical Flow with Chapters

Up to this point, I've encouraged you to write out of order using your mind map. I wanted you to get in the habit of writing. After writing all the content from the mind map sections, it's time to start putting some structure into your manuscript.

First, check the mind map and look for any topics you haven't covered. There may be topics you originally wanted to include, but haven't added to the manuscript. Revisit those topics to see if they still fit in the book. If you left some things out because they needed more research, decide if you want to do the research or exclude them.

Decide which of the book sections below are applicable to your manuscript.

- A Preface which describes the reasons you wrote the book

- An introduction that sets the stage, describing your point of view and who will benefit most from reading the book

- The main content in parts and chapters

- Chapter summaries

- A call to action - what you want the reader to do after they finish the book. Call to action examples are:

  - Visit your web site and sign up for your mailing list

  - Go to a landing page and sign up for a workshop

  - Visit a resource page to download templates or worksheets

  - Like your Facebook® business page or join a Facebook® group

  - Follow you on Twitter®

- An index

- A glossary

- Appendices

- Resources and required reading

## CHAPTERS PROVIDE THE STRUCTURE FOR YOUR BOOK

There are a few different ways you might want to organize your book: chronologically, in categories, or in a step-by-step process.

Let's look at each of them in more detail.

### Chronologically

This format style is well-suited for a memoir or autobiography. For example, a Rags to Riches story could start out with the humble beginnings of the main character, move to the struggles, trials, and challenges overcome along the way, and end with lessons learned and the success achieved.

### Categories

Books using this format style are typically tips books or quote books. For a book on stress relief, you could have categories of different types or causes of stress and the techniques to overcome them.

## Step-by-step process

Prescription books benefit from this format style. If your book aims to teach someone how to become a better golfer, you might start with the basics such as the correct stance or correct way to swing the club. Then move on to more complex ideas in subsequent chapters.

A variation of the step by step process is what I like to call the three act process, giving a nod to fiction books.

In the first part of the book, you outline why the reader needs the book and the problem they want to solve.

The second part of the book outlines the steps to resolve the problem.

The third part of the book tells the reader how to apply those steps to their personal situation.

You could have all three acts in each chapter. Let's say your book is about flower arranging. In the chapter on Japanese flower arrangement; you go through the three acts. In the chapter on orchids, you go through the three acts again because there are different problems related to that type of flower arrangement.

All of the formatting styles can be mixed and matched depending on what you're trying to accomplish in your book.

If your book doesn't lend itself to any of the formats described above, use something different as long as it's logical and won't confuse the reader.

**How to break up the content into logical chapters.**

A good place to start is with your mind map. Each section of the mind map is a self-contained topic which probably lends itself to becoming a chapter. It may make sense to combine one or more related topics into a single chapter.

Make the content accessible to different readers with short chapters. A reader should be able to go to the table of contents, find what they need and go straight to the chapter.

Each chapter should stand alone with a complete thought on a topic or sub-topic.

Your reader will be spending time thinking about the content and perhaps taking action at each step. The end of a chapter is a natural stopping point for the reader to review the chapter content and apply the lessons they learned.

**Hook the reader from the beginning of the book**

One thing non-fiction writers must give as much attention to as fiction writers is the first chapter. If you don't hook the reader at the beginning of the book, they may not stick around to read the rest of it. Start chapter one with a compelling story, a shocking statistic, a controversial idea, or the reader's aspiration.

Here are examples of the four ways to capture attention using books from my personal bookshelf:

1. **Tell a compelling story:** The *Little Book of Great Lines from Shakespeare* by Dick De Somogyi is a quotes book of lines from Shakespeare's plays. The book starts out with a compelling story about the moment in King Lear when the blind

Duke of Gloucester is led to the steep edge of Dover Cliff. De Somogyi uses the story to illustrate how Shakespeare's words are as powerful today as they were 400 years ago.

2. **State a shocking statistic:** I use this technique in *Maximum Occupancy*. I start the book by stating 60% of innkeepers depend on outside income to supplement the revenue generated from room bookings. The statistic sets the stage for the book's promise - to show B&B owners how to be profitable and self-sustaining with just the revenue from their inn.

3. **Raise a controversial idea:** A technique used in *First, Break All the Rules* by Marcus Buckingham and Curt Coffman. The controversial idea is that the greatest managers in the world don't have much in common. They're different sexes, races, and ages. Despite those differences, they do share one thing. Before they do anything else, they break all the rules of conventional wisdom.

4. **Describe the reader's aspiration:** In the book *Monday Morning Choices* by David Cottrell, he asks, "What if you could begin changing your

life simply by investing 20 minutes every Monday morning for 12 weeks?" If the reader wants to change, but felt it was too overwhelming, reading this statement is a huge incentive.

After you've captured the reader's attention, your goal for the rest of the book is to continue the momentum you've started in chapter one.

---

**Expert Author Action Step:**

Go back to the books you researched on Amazon and access the look inside feature. Note how those books start the first chapter to get some inspiration on how to begin your book.

---

Some ways to start subsequent chapters.

- A Quote. In *Monday Morning Choices*, every chapter starts with a quote pertinent to the chapter's topic. Each chapter ends with additional quotes related to the topic.

- A Story. The story could be a fable, an interview, or an excerpt from a case study.

- An Illustration. You could begin each chapter with a consistent illustration that's part of your book's brand, or an illustration or cartoon that changes depending on the chapter topic.

**Note: Quotes and illustrations can be used as section or chapter separators. The section title would be on a page by itself along with an illustration and/or quote.**

**Other formatting techniques for the text within each chapter:**

- **Callouts.** The expert author tip above is an example of a callout. It's a way to call attention to something very important within your chapter. Some books use a little graphic such as a light bulb or check mark. Others use a different typeface.

- **Ordered and unordered lists**. An ordered list is one that's numbered 1, 2, 3, 4, and 5. An unordered list contains bullets. This is a really good formatting technique to break up huge chunks of print. Writing apples, oranges, pears, grapes, and watermelon makes for a long sentence. Putting them in an unordered list makes them much easier to read:

- ○ apples
- ○ oranges
- ○ pears
- ○ grapes
- ○ watermelon

Learning points are especially effective in ordered and unordered lists. If the reader is skimming your content which a lot of readers do, this technique makes them pause to look at the list.

- **Action items or challenges**. I'm sure you've noticed the action items I've provided throughout this book. Action items encourage the reader to apply the principles you're teaching in the chapter.
- **Start or end a chapter with questions related to the chapter topic**. Questions help the reader deepen their understanding of the content.

As you think about the formatting techniques you'll use in your book, you may uncover gaps in content or research.

The book's format will have an impact on the size of your finished book as well. The industry standard count for one page is 250 words. If your first draft is 33,000 words it will translate to 150 pages.

All of the formatting techniques discussed above will add white space to the finished book. The white space will reduce the number of words needed to produce 150 pages.

For example, if your book contains quotes, the quotes will be in a different typeface with white space above and below the quote. Some authors put a quote at the beginning of each chapter and those quotes take up almost a quarter of the page.

Adding a glossary or suggested reading will increase the page count as well. As you can see, by adding interesting formatting techniques, you can decrease your writing workload while adding value for your readers.

> **Expert Author Action Step:** I've given you three examples of non-fiction books below. Visit Amazon and use the look inside feature to see what I'm describing.

1. *The Little Book of Talent: 52 Tips for Improving Your Skills* by Daniel Coyle. Mr. Coyle's book was on the New York Times Bestseller list. The book is divided into three sections. Each section starts with an illustration related to the individual chapters. Each tip is accompanied by an illustration. Some tips are covered on a single page. Others take two or three pages to complete. If you're writing a tip book and each tip takes up two pages, a book with 50 tips would have 100 pages.

2. The Chicken Soup for the Soul series. Chicken Soup for the Soul started out as just one book. Now there are versions for Women, Men, Teenagers, Students, and Animal Lovers. All of the books are written in an anthology format. Multiple authors contribute stories based on a theme. Those stories are then compiled by the authors to create the book. Just as we saw with the tip book, some stories are only half a page long. Others are two pages or three pages.

3. *Awaken the giant within: How to take immediate control of your mental, emotional, physical, and financial destiny* by Tony Robbins. It's a prescription book.

Any time you see how-to in the title, that's typically a prescription. The author is telling you how to fix or improve something.

**Note:** Questions and challenges are an opportunity for you to write a companion book. You can compile all of the questions and turn them into a workbook.

It will give the reader space to answer all of the questions in one place.

An example of this is *The Four Agreements*, a New York Times bestseller by Don Miguel Ruiz.

Mr. Ruiz wrote a companion book titled *The Four Agreements Companion book: Using the four agreements to master the dream of your life* (a Toltec wisdom book).

The workbook contains additional information from the author, deeper insight, and practical ways for the reader to apply the learning from the original book.

---

**Expert Author Action Step**

Decide on your chapter and page layout and adjust your word count estimate as needed.

---

# CHAPTER 16

## Choose a Typeface Combination

Today, people use the words font and typeface inter-changeably, but typeface is a printing term and font is a computer term.

A font is a combination of the typeface and the size of the letters in the typeface.

When you select the font Arial 14 in your word pro-cessing program, Arial is the typeface and 14 is the size of the type in points.

### Why is typography important for your book?

Think about the distinctive typeface used in the Coca Cola logo. It's recognizable all over the world and evokes a feeling about their brand.

In the same way, the typeface of your book will evoke a certain feeling in the reader. The typeface should complement the book's style, be suitable for large blocks of text, and easy to read. Your book's typeface is a subtle part of your branding.

Your choice of typeface is another way to elevate your book from the ranks of the sloppily published and into the realm of professionally published books.

**Font Families**

When I open the font folder on my computer and look at Adobe Garamond Pro, I see four separate typefaces: regular, bold, bold italic, and italic. This is called a font family. In my word processing software, when I click the italics icon, the program uses the font file Adobe Garamond Pro Italic.

It's very important that your manuscript be written using a font family. Otherwise, it may not translate properly during the professional print process. An italic may come out too faint to read or a bold may not be smooth.

You can easily check this on your computer by going to the fonts folder. The fonts folder is found in different locations depending on your computer and operating system.

I recommend an Internet search on how to find the fonts folder for your particular computer and operating system. Make sure the folder contains the entire typeface family.

**Two types of typefaces - Serif and Sans Serif**

There are two types of typefaces. One is called Serif and the other is called Sans Serif.

Serif simply means it has little decorative edges on the letters. Serif typefaces originated in the early days of printing when books were written by hand.

The pens used by the writers created letters similar to calligraphy, thin on one side and thick on the other. Writers would use the pens to put flourishes or loops at the ends of the letters.

**An example of Serif and Sans Serif fonts:**

Serif font: Book Antiqua

San Serif font: Century Gothic

As you can see, the Serif font, Book Antiqua has a different feel from the Sans Serif font, Century Gothic.

Also note that even though both lines are written in 12 point size, the Book Antiqua font is much smaller and takes up less room on the page.

There are thousands of typefaces but not all of them are appropriate for books.

Unlike in marketing, where you want to stand out from the crowd, the inside of your book should look like all of the professionally produced books sold by the New York publishing houses.

I recommend choosing typefaces from a list which I'll share later in this chapter.

You will choose two typefaces for your book interior. A Sans Serif typeface will be used for chapter and section titles, headings, and sub-headings.

A Serif typeface will be used for the text or body of your chapters.

Using two different typefaces provides contrast and interest. The typefaces need to complement each other.

You don't want one to be ornate and the other one to be minimalistic.

For this book, I chose the serif typeface Book Antiqua for the body of the chapters and paired it with the sans serif typeface Verdana for titles and headings. If you like the combination, feel free to use them in your book.

Stay away from commonly used word processing fonts like Arial, Courier, Comic Sans MS, and Times New Roman. These fonts are either overused or not suitable for books.

Following, in no particular order, are other recommended typeface combinations. These typefaces have been used by award winning and bestselling nonfiction books.

You may already have some of the typefaces on your computer. Any typeface/font not available on your computer can be found on the internet. Some fonts/typefaces may require you to purchase them in order to use them commercially such as in a book project.

**Sans Serif Typefaces/Fonts to be used for titles and headings**

- Gill Sans
- Helvetica
- Futura
- League Gothic
- Poppl-Laudatio
- Myriad Pro
- Verdana
- Helvetica Neue
- Trajan
- Franklin Gothic
- Baskerville

**Serif typefaces/fonts to be used for body text**

- Garamond
- Book Antiqua
- Bookman
- Minion
- Georgia
- Adobe Caslon
- Palatino
- Goody

- Baskerville
- Century
- Hasler

If you're worried about picking a typeface combination that will look good, I'll make it even easier for you.

There are some classic typeface combinations. I've listed three below. If you pick one of these, you can't go wrong:

- Myriad Pro sans serif for titles and Adobe Caslon serif for text
- Helvetica Neue  sans serif for titles and Garamond serif for text
- Poppl-Laudatio sans serif for titles and Minion serif for text.

Another way to pick a typeface combination is to refer back to the research you did at the library and your local bookstore.

There's nothing wrong with finding a typeface combination used by a NY Times bestseller and using the same combination in your book.

Take a picture of several words on one of the pages and a picture of the chapter title. Upload the pictures to:

http://www.myfonts.com/WhatTheFont/

The site will give its best guess as to the typeface.

After you've picked out a few typeface combinations that look promising, you'll want to test them out.

1. Open a new word processing document. Copy and paste a section of your book's manuscript into the document.
2. Change the text and titles to the typeface combination you want to test using font size 12.
3. Repeat this exercise with the other typeface combinations you're considering.

**What about point size?**

Point size, is the vertical measurement of the lettering in a font. There are approximately 72 points in one inch. As point size increases, the size of the type increases accordingly. This means a page produced in 14 point type will have fewer words than a page produced with 12 point type.

See the difference in the example below:

This is Gandhi Serif using 12 point type

# This is Gandhi Serif using 14 point type

The 14 point sentence takes up a lot more room on the page than the 12 point sentence.

The point size and typeface give your page a specific look and feel. You want to ensure the typeface combination is consistent with your topic and the feeling you want to portray.

As a rule of thumb, choose an 11 or 12 point typeface for the body text and a 14 point typeface for headings and sub-headings. If your chapter titles are on a page by themselves, you could choose an even larger point size.

When you tested the typeface combinations, you probably noticed the print was a different size depending on the typeface, even though you selected a point size of 12 for all of them.

Some authors use typeface/point size as a way to increase the number of pages in their book. I don't recommend this tactic. There's a danger of having your book look amateurish if the point size is very large.

A better way to increase the size of your book is to use the formatting techniques we discussed such as creating lists, including illustrations and charts, or creating call-outs and summaries.

**Note:** Typography isn't important in the eBook version of your book. Today's eReaders give the buyer the ability to change the font when they read.

In fact, if you have a Kindle like I do, Amazon has created its own font called Bookerly, which you can make the default. Every time you open a book, regardless of the original typeface, you will view the content in Bookerly.

> **Expert Author Action Item:** Pick a typeface combination and convert your manuscript. Use the serif font for the entire manuscript. Then go back through and change the titles to your chosen Sans Serif font.

You can easily change the default typeface in Scrivener. For the Windows version go to: Tools > Options... > Formatting.

Pressing 'A' will bring up font options. Select your font. Now any new text will be written using that font.

To convert existing text go to: Documents > Convert > Formatting to Default Text Style.

*Linda Griffin*

# CHAPTER 17

## Finalize the Book Title

Now that the first draft of your manuscript is almost complete, it's time to finalize the book title.

There are rules for titles and there are no rules for titles. That may seem contradictory but let me explain.

When I researched the methodology for creating best-selling book titles, I found many bestselling books don't follow the rules.

I concluded that marketing ultimately determines whether a book is going to sell or not.

Having a great title doesn't automatically mean the book will sell. By the same token, a not so great title could sell very well if it's marketed effectively by the author.

An intriguing book title will have a better chance of at-tracting your ideal reader. After all, the book title is the first thing a buyer will see when they're searching for something to read.

The book title should:

- Capture the essence of what the reader will gain when they read the book.

- Be readily visible and readable in the thumbnail version so that it doesn't disappear when viewed in an online store.

- Be easy to remember so friends and family can recommend it to others.

- Give your unique spin on the topic. If your book's topic is one that's been written about a lot such as travel or leadership, think about how you can highlight a new aspect of the topic using your title.

- Match the style of the contents. If you write about the book topic using a serious tone, a lighthearted tone, or a quirky tone, the title should match the tone.

- Fit easily on the cover of the book along with any images you plan to use.

You want friends and family to recommend your book to others. If your topic is controversial, will you feel comfortable telling them the title? If you plan to build a business around your book with speaking and consulting, will the title fit your brand?

**Your book title will be used:**

- By buyers searching for a solution to a problem

- As a marketing tool

- As part of your branding on other marketing materials such as bookmarks and posters

- On your author/book website

- On presentation slides

- On audio book covers

- On workbook covers

- In social media posts

**The Expert Author formula for non-fiction book titles**

While there's no set formula for non-fiction book titles, I've developed one formula anyone can use when writing a book that solves the problem.

**Title:** the reader's aspiration

**Sub-title:** the benefit to the reader

**Optional:** the target audience

Here's how I used the formula in *Maximum Occupancy: How Smart Innkeepers Put Heads in Beds in Every Season:*

**Title:** Maximum Occupancy

**Sub-title:** Put heads in beds in every season

**Optional:** Smart Innkeepers

This formula works because it lets the ideal reader know as soon as they see the cover, the problem the book aims to solve and the benefit they will gain.

When my ideal reader, innkeepers, look at the cover, they know it will address their aspiration to maximize their occupancy rate and solve the problem of how to put heads in beds in every season.

I chose the same approach with *Book Smart: The Ninety Day Guide to Writing and Self-publishing for Busy Entrepreneurs, Business Owners, and Corporate Professionals.*

**Title:** Book Smarts

**Sub-title:** The ninety day guide to writing and self-publishing

**Optional:** Busy Entrepreneurs, Business Owners, and Corporate Professionals

If you're struggling with the title for your book, I recommend hiring someone on Fiverr.com to write some book titles or taglines. You may not get a perfect book title but they will give you a starting point.

If you already have a signature program, process, or procedure, consider using the process name as the title with an explanatory sub-title.

**Title considerations**

**Perform an Internet Search**

As you brainstorm a list of titles to consider, enter them into an Internet search. A title can't be copyrighted, so you may find a book with the exact same title you want to use.

While it's not a copyright problem, it can be a marketing problem. If someone is searching for your title and two books come up in the results with the same title, which one will they pick?

If one of those titles was written by someone famous than you, chances are the reader will pick the book written by someone whose name they recognize.

The second reason to search your title is to see what other types of results come up. You don't want to be associated with something X-rated, embarrassing, or offensive.

**Read the title out loud.**

You want to ensure your title is easy to understand if it's spoken aloud during a radio interview.

There's a men's store name that baffled me for years. They ran a radio commercial during my commute to work.

I always thought the name of the store was the letter K, the letter N, the letter G that is KNG, because that's what I heard.

It wasn't until I saw a TV ad that I realized the store name was K&G. Try saying KNG and K&G out loud and see for yourself. If there are words in your book title that could be misunderstood if someone hears it on the radio, pick some other words.

**Consider including a number in the title.**

People love numbers because they put a value to what they're getting in the book.

**Use a word that evokes an emotional response** such as "why", "how", "new", or "secret".

> **Expert Author Action: Brainstorm four or five versions of your title, research them and pick the best one.**

*Linda Griffin*

# CHAPTER 18

## Edit the First Draft

After you've written all of the content for the sections and chapters, it's time to self-edit the first draft.

Put the manuscript away for a few days. This will put some distance between yourself and your work. You'll be able to look at it with fresh eyes when you start to edit.

When you come back to your manuscript, complete these steps:

1. Run a spell check and grammar check from your writing tool to eliminate obvious errors.
2. Print the manuscript using double spacing and wide margins on the top, bottom, and sides. You'll need the space to write notes in preparation for making corrections.

3. Place the manuscript in a three-ring binder to make it easy to flip back and forth as you're working.

4. Sit down in a quiet place, and read your manuscript out loud to put yourself in the reader's place and get a sense of how the words flow. I've found my pets to be great listeners! The reason you want to read your manuscript out loud as opposed to reading it in your head is words sound different when you read them out loud. You can more easily catch errors. Check for grammar and spelling because your writing tool won't catch everything. The more errors you can catch as you're doing your own self-edit, the less work your editor will have to do.

5. As you read, make notes in the margins of things you want to change. Resist the urge to do this mark-up on your computer. Stay in Reader Mode. Read and make notations throughout the entire manuscript before going back to the computer to complete the edits. Set aside several blocks of time to avoid fatigue. Use the blocks of time you had allocated to your writing and re-purpose them for editing.

6.  Review the book's table of contents and ensure the topics flow logically from a beginner's point of view. There are things you take for granted because of your experience but don't assume your reader will know them. In particular, pay attention to acronyms and insider jargon that could confuse the reader. I was working with a client recently over the phone helping her to setup a monthly newsletter using the MailChimp app. I asked her to look at the menu at the bottom of the screen and she couldn't see it although it seemed obvious to me. It wasn't until we walked through every section of the screen that she finally said, "Oh, now I see the menu!"

7.  Note any content you want to move to a different chapter or eliminate.

8.  Check for repetitive/favorite words you may have used too many times and reduce them. I like to use the word 'great' so I'm always on the lookout for how many times I use it in a writing project. I have to consciously make sure I'm not saying great in every other sentence because it will quickly annoy my readers.

As a first time author, you probably won't be happy with your first draft but don't get discouraged. It's all part of the process.

If you find your manuscript requires a major re-write, stop and don't complete the editing process. You run the risk of doing double work by cleaning up language that might be deleted from the manuscript after you correct the structural changes.

Come back to this chapter when you've completed the rewrite and go through the self-editing steps.

After you've marked up the first draft, go back to your writing app and complete the edits.

Check the word count to make sure you didn't remove too much content. If that's the case, consider adding additional content in the form of case studies, interviews, tips, or checklists to get the word count back into the desired range.

---

**Expert Author Action Steps:**

1.  Print out the manuscript double spaced with wide margins and place in a three ring binder
2.  Read the manuscript out loud and mark-up the required changes on the hard copy document
3.  If your manuscript requires a major rewrite, contact me for help.
4.  Take your manuscript back to your writing tool and make the edits
5.  After you make the changes, don't look at your work for at least a week.

---

Congratulations! You've just completed the hardest part of your book project.

# CHAPTER 19

## Engage Beta Readers

After completing the first draft edit, it's smart to get feedback from real readers who are in your ideal target market.

I come from the information technology world. For several years, I was a software development manager. One of my teams was responsible for creating complex applications used to manage and operate an automated warehouse.

After the development team had thoroughly tested the updates internally, we brought in a small group of business people, called Beta Testers who would ultimately use the application in real life.

They were given the user guide, access to the application and told to use the system as they would in their day to day jobs.

The Beta Testers brought a real world perspective to the project. If the user guide wasn't clear, they would uncover it. If they hit the wrong set of keys and an unexpected result happened, it would highlight a problem or identify a need for better documentation.

I would never consider going live with a new software application without completing a beta test.

A beta test gave us the opportunity to make the finished application more user-friendly. The testers identified things we didn't consider because we were too close to the project.

Sometimes, a step would be left out of the user guide because we made the assumption everyone would know how to perform a specific activity.

Just like software developers, you've made some assumptions about the knowledge your reader is bringing to the book.

A Beta Reader is someone from your book's target market who will read the manuscript as if they had bought it off the shelf.

A Beta Reader will uncover things you didn't consider or things that need to be tweaked in order to make your book more readable and more useful.

When looking for Beta Readers, pick two or three people who fit your ideal reader profile. I recommend staying away from family or close friends because they may be afraid to give you feedback for fear of hurting your feelings.

If you're writing a book about stress relief for corporate women, pick beta readers from your female corporate contacts.

Other places to look for beta readers are your writing group, book club, social media contacts, or reading group. There are online beta reading groups as well. Goodreads.com is a great place to find them.

Give your beta readers permission to give you honest feedback and make it easy for them to respond.

You can thank them later with a signed copy of the published book or by adding their names to the acknowledgments page in the book.

Making sure you get the beta reader feedback returned on time to fit your publishing schedule is very important.

Here are some suggestions on how to make getting feedback easy for you and your beta readers:

- Give your beta readers a specific date to return their feedback, giving yourself a buffer before you need to send your manuscript to the editor/proofreader. Two weeks should be sufficient. Don't assume they can meet the deadline. Ask them to confirm. If a beta reader doesn't make the deadline, give them a gentle reminder a few days later. If they don't respond, move on.

- Send a PDF file or printed manuscript depending on their preference. Include a cover letter or email containing the book description, the problem your book is solving, and the target reader.

- Provide a format for the feedback to make it easy for them and easy for you to compare the feedback. My personal preference for receiving feedback is a questionnaire. With a questionnaire, you can compare apples to apples and easily make a decision on the feedback you will incorporate in your final draft. You can create a questionnaire as a simple Word document or use surveymonkey.com to create an online questionnaire.

- Instruct them to read the book, not edit the book. Let them know the book will go to a professional editor and you're not asking them to find typos. If they happen to run across a typo, they can indicate it but you want them to read the manuscript's content to determine whether it provides value.

**Here are some sample questions to include when asking your beta readers for feedback:**

1. Did the book adequately address the problem identified in the book description?

2. Did you experience any breakthroughs in thinking? If so, please describe.

3. Identify any areas of the book that weren't clear or were confusing.

4. What did you like best about the book?

5. How could I improve the content?

6. What was your biggest take-away from the book?

7. If you saw the book in a bookstore, would you buy it?

Remember you're the final arbiter. This is your book. At the end of the day, only you know your vision. You don't have to change anything if you don't agree.

Just ensure you're being realistic. You aren't your ideal reader. You know your subject inside and out but your readers don't.

If you've done a good job of picking your beta readers, they will be representative of the type of person who will buy your book. Take their feedback seriously. If the same comment is made by multiple people, you need to pay attention.

> **Expert Author Action:** Send your manuscript to two or three beta readers. Collect their feedback.

# CHAPTER 20

## Polish the Diamond

After receiving beta reader feedback, you're going to work on the second draft of your manuscript getting it ready to submit for professional editing, proofreading and printing.

Working on the second draft is what I call "polishing the diamond". When a diamond comes out of the mine, it looks like a dull and uninteresting rock.

The rough diamond is cut, polished, and put into a beautiful setting before selling it to its ultimate owner. Now the diamond sparkles and shines brilliantly.

You're going to do the same thing with your manuscript. You'll cut away unnecessary words, make sure the flow is logical, and eliminate gaps in content.

Completing this step successfully is one of the things that separates a professionally written book from one that looks amateurish.

First, read through the comments you received from the beta readers and decide what, if anything you want to change based on their feedback.

You're going to repeat some of the steps you took when editing the first draft. In my experience, you can't edit enough. Even traditionally published books with an entire publishing machine supporting them often contain errors. As an independent author, it's imperative you give as much attention to detail as possible to produce a high quality book.

1. Read the sections referenced by the beta readers and make changes as needed.

2. Decide whether to split or combine chapters. Consider adding more content to very short chapters.

3. Check the length of paragraphs. They should be three to five sentences long. If they're any longer, the reader's eye gets tired. Remember, every time you start a new thought, start a new paragraph.

4. Check sentence structure. Your sentences should ebb and flow, some longer, some shorter. If all of the sentences are the same length, meaning they have the same number of words, they start to sound repetitive and quite boring. Repetition is good for kid's books but not so much for adults. Create a mixture of short sentences, medium sentences, and slightly longer sentences to keep your text interesting. If you write in a conversational tone, this should happen automatically. Just make sure you don't over edit and take away the variety.

5. Increase confidence with editing apps. I use two editing apps which can be found at Grammarly.com and ProWritingAid.com. These apps are designed to eliminate errors and enhance your writing. Both offer free versions but in order to review your entire manuscript, you'll need to sign up for one of the paid versions. Using an editing app is optional. If you feel your self-editing is good enough to go to a professional editor to complete the process, skip this step.

6. Ensure your chapters end at an appropriate summary level. If you're giving the reader instructions, don't stop in the middle of an instruction set.

---

**Expert Author Action Step: Complete the edits on the second draft.**

# Part 3

# Publish Your Book

*"Nothing stinks like a pile of unpublished writing."*

-–Sylvia Plath

*Linda Griffin*

# CHAPTER 21

## Getting Ready to Publish

You've incorporated the suggestions from your beta readers. You've completed a second draft. You may be tempted to move right on to publishing, but I encourage you to engage a professional editor.

The goal I laid out for you at the beginning of this book was to create a finished product you would be proud to place beside any bestseller produced by a fancy New York publishing house.

To ensure a top quality book, there are a few more steps you need to take:

- Have your manuscript professionally edited and proofread
- Include industry standard book components
- Acquire an ISBN number

- Incorporate a professionally designed book interior layout

- Get a professionally produced cover design

Currently, there's an air freshener commercial running on television. A mom walks into her teenage son's bedroom and asks if he's expecting guests. When he says yes, Mom tells him the room smells horrible. Teenage son is confused.

The announcer reminds us when we smell something continuously, our brain filters it out. When someone new enters the room, they notice the bad odors right away.

Errors in grammar, punctuation, etc. are just like those odors. We're so close to our manuscript that we read the words we intended to write as opposed to what we actually wrote.

I encouraged you to read your manuscript out loud during the self-editing process. Reading aloud uncovers errors you might skip over when you're reading silently. I also encouraged you to use some of the online editing tools.

If you followed my recommendations during the self-editing process, your manuscript will be as clean as possible prior to sending it to a professional editor.

Editor fees can be based on word count, page count or at an hourly rate. A good self-edit ensures you're not wasting their time and your money by giving them a manuscript riddled with errors.

You may be tempted to skip the expense of hiring a professional editor, but it's important to have a trained editor review your manuscript if you want to minimize errors in your finished book.

Here are the types of editing I've found most valuable for expert authors:

A **developmental editor** analyzes the structure and flow of a book. They look for inconsistencies in logic and tone.

If you received feedback from beta readers expressing a lot of confusion or lack of understanding, there may be a problem with the book's structure/outline or with your writing. Your manuscript may need significant re-writing or re-structuring.

A developmental editor will correct errors in the book's outline and work with you through the re-write of each chapter. If your manuscript requires this type of re-write, you should also consider hiring a ghost writer.

It can be very discouraging and time consuming to un-cover a major problem at this point in the book project. At ExpertAuthor411.com/work-with-me, I offer a manuscript audit to help you decide if the work can be salvaged without going to the extreme of hiring a de-velopmental editor.

A **copy editor** reviews the form of your writing as op-posed to the content of your writing. They ensure it conforms to the appropriate writing style manual.

They review and correct errors in grammar, punctua-tion, capitalization, sentence structure, and syntax.

They'll look for inconsistencies and make suggestions to correct repetitive words and phrases. This is the type of editing I recommend for all expert authors.

A **proofreader** is the last person to see the book before printing copies in volume quantities. I think of them as quality control. They ensure the front and back matter, photos, and captions are correctly placed.

They check for missing pages along with consistent typeface use for headings and sub-headings. They make sure pages and chapters end smoothly without dangling words.

Proofreading will give your readers an easy button. It will be easy for them to understand perfectly punctuated text.

**Expert Author Action:** Get quotes from two or three copy editors. Choose an editor and email the manuscript to them in Microsoft Word format.

Compile your document from Scrivener into Microsoft WORD format. Use the non-fiction manuscript format from the compile drop down menu. Scrivener will compile the manuscript and export the file to your computer.

**Note: When comparing editing estimates, ensure you're comparing apples to apples. Some copy editors**

quote prices based on word count. Others quote prices based on page count. Professional editors consider a page to be 250 words.   Check to see if the editor bundles other services, such as proof reading in their quoted rates.

---

**Expert Author Action: Review the changes recommended by the editor and update your manuscript as needed.** In general, you should accept all the changes recommended by the editor. You hired them for their experience in grammar, syntax, and clarity.  Trust them as an expert in their field.

---

### A note about Copyright and ISBN

**Should you register a copyright?**

Your book is under copyright protection as soon as you complete the work, whether you publish it or not.

You will include a copyright statement in the front matter of the finished book. Depending on your personal preference, you can formally register the copyright to make it easier to litigate if someone steals your work.

Copyright rules vary from country to country so check with the copyright office in your region for more detail. In the U.S. visit copyright.gov/registration

---

**Expert Author Action: (Optional) Register a copyright, based on your personal preference.**

---

**Should you purchase an ISBN?**

When I attended Book Expo, the national conference for the book publishing industry, I asked the question of the experts and here's what I've determined: If you want your book to be ordered by any retail outlet, bookstore, or library you must have an ISBN.

An ISBN identifies a specific version of a book in the retail book distribution system. ISBNs are used by retail outlets and libraries to order and track book inventory.

If you want to sell your book at brick and mortar stores such as Barnes and Noble, or Walmart, you must have an ISBN. Some event organizers, writing contests, and industry book review magazines may require an ISBN to consider your book.

By purchasing an ISBN, your book will be included in **Books in Print**, the world's largest catalog of books. **Books in Print** is licensed to all major search engines, bookstores and libraries.

If you plan to sell your book on Amazon, it will also require an ISBN Number, however, if you use Amazon's publishing platform, Create Space, they include several options for purchasing ISBN numbers as part of their publishing package. The fee ranges from free to $99.

If you choose any of the Amazon Create Space options, they will register your title at Books in Print. There is one caveat to the Create Space ISBN: if you use the free option, Create Space will be listed as your publisher.

This could impact a retail outlet's decision to purchase your title, either because of assumptions about quality or because they don't want to pay their competitor – Amazon for the title.

**My conclusion:** Your decision boils down to how you plan to use the book. If you plan to sell your book only on your own website, or in person at events you don't need an ISBN.

If you think you will use any of the traditional outlets, request trade reviews, or enter contests, I recommend making the investment.

Bowker is the official source for ISBNs in the United States. As of this writing, one ISBN will require an investment of $125 and you will need one ISBN for every version of your book.

The print version will require one ISBN and the eBook version of the same title will require a different ISBN.

At the time of this writing, you can get a block of ten ISBNs for $295. If you're not in the U.S. visit isbn-international.org to find the registration agency in your country.

There are other companies who sell ISBNs. Some independent publishing or hybrid publishing companies include an ISBN as part of the publishing package.

Do your homework before you sign up with one of the third-party sites selling ISBNs.

If you don't purchase from the official ISBN Agency or one of its channel partners, you run the risk of your book not being identified correctly.

That can impact the ability of your book to be found in the publishing industry supply chain.

The next question is whether to purchase one ISBN or a block of ISBN numbers. If you plan to write one book, and only one version of that book, you will need one ISBN.

That's probably not the case if you're planning to use your book to build authority and act as a lead generation tool. You will want to have a print version, an eBook version, and potentially an audio version. That will require three ISBNs.

In my book coaching program, I encourage my clients to write a book that focuses on solving one big problem in their niche. The narrow focus facilitates getting the book written and published in a shorter period of time and it leaves the door open for them to share more of their wisdom in later books.

If they write just one more book, that's three more ISBNs. Now you see why the most popular package is the block of ten ISBNs for $295.

One last thing to consider: In the book industry, books are published by companies, not individuals. When Bowker issues an ISBN or block of ISBNs, they will request the name of the publisher and the imprint name, if applicable.

Some publishing companies produce books targeted to more than one marketing segment or they have acquired other publishing companies.

In those cases, they create what's called a publishing imprint. It's a trade name used to create a separate brand identity and distinguish between different types of books or market segments.

For example, the publisher Random House produces mass market paperbacks under the imprint Bantam Books and literary classics under the Random House imprint.

As a self-publishing expert author, you have several options for creating your publishing company and imprint. If you're a business owner, you can simply use an imprint which would be owned by your company.

For example, Cheree Warrick chose her company name, The Profit Partner, LLC. as the publisher for her book, while my client, Cyndy Porter chose to use the imprint STS Publishing which is owned by her company, Cyndy Porter Style and Photography.

If you're a sole proprietor, you can register the publishing company using your name or an imprint. Please consult your tax advisor before making a final decision.

---

**Expert Author Action: Purchase a block of ISBNs**

---

# CHAPTER 22

## The Expert Author Bio

Your author bio will go in two places - a long version in the back matter of your book and a short version on the back cover.

The author bio helps to establish your credibility and authority. It's a marketing tool to help you sell books.

Keep your target reader in mind as you're writing the bio. Your goal is to gain their trust and justify the investment they will make in purchasing and reading your book.

The short version for the back cover should be one or two sentences that establish trust in the reader's mind. Mention training, accolades, or experience to demonstrate your expertise.

The back cover bio will also be used by the media. Reporters or podcast hosts may not have time to read the entire book. Scanning the back cover and author bio could generate enough interest for them to contact you about an interview or article.

The longer version of your bio will go in the book's back matter. It should be two or three short paragraphs.

A checklist for the long version of the author bio:

1. Write the bio in the third person. Less is more. This is not the time to share your entire life's history.
2. Quickly establish your credibility by stating any professional qualifications, certifications, or education related to the book's topic. Mention the titles of other books you've written, your website, and any personal achievements that apply.
3. Include your job title and/or the name of your business if it's relevant to the book's topic.
4. Include any awards you've received, or related firsthand experience.

5. Mention any interviews from radio, TV, or large Internet authority sites such as the Huffington Post.

6. Mention your city and state. Local event planners, bookstores, and journalists are always looking for home town people of interest. If you live in a small town you may want to use the nearest larger city as your home town. I live in Ashburn, Va. which isn't well known, but when I say I live in the Washington D.C. metro area, it's instantly recognizable.

7. Add a few personal details such as hobbies.

8. Add a call to action asking the reader to sign up for your mailing list or offering a special download for book purchasers. End with one personal fact about yourself.

9. Both the back cover copy and the author bio are major pieces of marketing collateral. If you don't feel comfortable with copywriting techniques, this is the time to hire a professional copywriter to complete them. As a trained copywriter, I'm able to offer those services to clients in my book coaching programs.

**Expert Author Action:** Write your author bio short and long versions.

# CHAPTER 23

## Style the Book Interior Layout

When formatting the inside layout of your book, the first thing you need to decide is the trim size. Trim sizes are typically shown in inches, length by width. I recommend using one of the standard book sizes of 5.5" x 8.5", 6" x 9", or 8.5" x 11".

These sizes don't require special paper or set-up at the printing companies. They're also the sizes of books people are used to seeing in libraries and book stores.

After you decide the trim size, you can move on to the interior design.

Have you ever put a T-shirt on backwards? I've done it a few times when I'm rushing to get dressed in the dark. I've even walked around for a few minutes with the shirt on backwards but something didn't feel right.

Then I realized what was making me feel uncomfortable – the shirt was on backwards!

A professionally produced book has a certain feel to the reader. They probably won't notice when it's right but will feel uncomfortable when it's wrong.

That uncomfortable feeling is undoubtedly because the interior of the book wasn't formatted properly.

Interior book design elements include:

- The overall page layout , the margins, and page numbers
- Typeface(fonts and type sizes) for chapter titles, headings and body text
- Graphic elements such as images, call-outs, and charts
- The typesetting of each page so that text flows properly from line to line and page to page
- Industry standard components. I've included a list below. You'll notice some components are optional and depend on the type of book you're writing.

**FRONT MATTER (numbered using lower case Roman numerals i, ii, iii, iv, etc.)**

- Half title page (containing only the title)

- Blank (or could list Also by the author, also in the series etc.)

- Title page containing the title, subtitle, author and publisher

- Copyright containing the edition information, publication information, printing history, legal notices, and ISBN number. The copyright notice can take several formats. You can show it as © Copyright [year] [author name] or © Copyright [year] [publisher name].

- Dedication

- Table of contents listing all of the parts and chapters of the book

- List of illustrations (optional)

- List of tables (optional)

- Foreword (optional): Written by someone who is not the author, usually someone who lends credibility to the book. It's signed by the person who wrote the Foreword

- Preface (optional): Written by the author. Describes why the author decided to write the book, the book's scope, and who will benefit the most from the book

## MAIN BODY OF THE BOOK (numbered using Arabic numerals 1,2,3,4, etc.)

- Introduction: Puts the book in context. Describes the purpose and goals of the book
- Book Text: Includes sections, parts, and chapters
- Afterword (optional): Comments from the author that add context about the creation of the book

## BACK MATTER

- ☐ Appendix/Appendices (optional)
- ☐ Glossary(optional)
- ☐ Acknowledgments: Thank the people who helped you make the book possible
- ☐ Bibliography(optional)
- ☐ List of contributors(optional)
- ☐ Index(optional)

- [ ] Call to Action
- [ ] Author Bio

There are several options for getting the interior of your book formatted properly:

- Do it yourself. I'm listing this option only for the sake of clarity. I strongly caution you against attempting to design the book interior from scratch on your own. Unless you want to learn about running heads, widows, orphans, gutters, and a host of other confusing terminology, don't try this at home!

- Use a professional book design template. This is an upscale version of do it yourself. A professional has thought through the details so you don't have to worry about them. You copy and paste your content into the template. If you or your assistant are proficient in Microsoft Word or Adobe InDesign, using a template can be cost effective. If you decide to take this route, I recommend bookdesigntemplates.com. The templates were created by Joel Friedlander, a respected book designer.

- Hire a professional book designer. Custom book designers work closely with you to choose typefaces and a layout that provides synergy with the overall theme of your message. I recommend you make the investment to outsource the design work to a professional.

> **Expert Author Action: Send the manuscript to a professional book designer for interior formatting.**

# CHAPTER 24

## Create a Killer Book Cover

People do judge a book by its cover. It's the first thing potential readers will see and the first decision point your reader will use to determine whether they'll buy or not.

Book covers evoke an emotional response and you want yours to make a positive one. Some people aren't willing to start reading a book if they don't like the cover.

I strongly urge you to hire a professional cover designer even if you have an idea about how you want your cover to look. A cover designer can take your ideas and transform them into magic!

When hiring a cover designer, ensure they produce covers for physical print books. Some designers specialize in eBook covers. eBooks don't have a spine like printed books and won't work for our purposes.

You can collaborate very closely with your cover designer or give them a general idea and let them use their creativity to come up with a design.

Alan Rinzler, a famous book editor, says your book cover is a unique face. Thousands of books have been written on leadership. If you pick up any two leadership books, they're going to look different based on the author's view of the topic.

**Front cover considerations**

**1. It needs to look good in thumbnail size.**

Most people will search for your book on Amazon or one of the other online retail sites. Your book cover will be represented by a thumbnail sized image. For this reason, use an easy to read typeface and an image that won't become blurry when reduced to the smaller size.

You don't have to use a graphic, photo, or clip art on the front cover. You can eliminate an image and use an interesting typeface. John Maxwell's book, *The 5 levels of Leadership* doesn't use a graphic.

Pay attention to the colors you plan to use and ensure the cover is still legible if printed in black and white (really shades of gray).

## 2. Author Name

If you normally use a nickname such as Pat instead of Patricia, consider that when deciding what author name to use on your book. If everyone knows you as Pat, that's the name they'll use when searching for your book.

Be consistent. Use the same variation of your name across your entire author platform such as your website, your author page on Amazon, and your social media accounts so that it becomes part of your brand.

## 3. Don't be too literal

I struggle with this myself. Due to my left brain dominance, I tend to be very literal. In a TED Talk® given by book designer Chip Kidd, he makes fun of a lot of things related to designing books, but includes practical advice as well. One of his examples uses an apple as an illustration.

If your book is about apples, you either want to have a picture of an apple, or the word apple on your book cover. You don't want to have the word apple superimposed upon a picture of an apple. That's too literal.

## 4. Make it shareable

Use a graphic that will look good when people share it on Facebook®, pin it on Pinterest®, or post it on Instagram.

## Back cover considerations

On the back cover, you'll have room for approximately 150 to 200 words. The back cover should give a short reason why someone might want to buy the book.

Start with your one paragraph book description. Follow up with three to five bullet points describing what the reader will learn. Alternatively, you could include a couple of book endorsements.

At the bottom of the back cover, put a short author bio and a professional author photo. Add your website URL to the end of the author bio. The author photo should be the same one you use with all of your marketing and branding.

**Other items to put on the back cover:**

- ISBN and ISBN bar code. Some book cover designers will create the bar code as part of their services.
- The retail price. Review the market research you did on competitive titles and set the price in the range for similar titles.

**Pricing considerations:**

If you want to get your book into as many hands as possible, one of the important factors you need to consider is the cover price.

Amazon and other online book distributors have set an expectation for what a printed book and an eBook is worth. Take this into account when setting the retail price.

The retail price is what goes on your book cover, however, one of the advantages you have as a self-publisher is the ability to sell the book at a discount in order to attract more readers.

For example, you can run a short term special during your book launch or give a discount to customers who purchase your book at a conference.

When you did your initial market research, you wrote down the page counts and prices of both the paperback and eBook versions of the books you found on your topic. When readers browse Amazon for your key-words, other author's books will come back in the search results.

Your book's price needs to be in the average price range for other books of similar page count and subject matter; otherwise, it puts a question in the reader's mind.

If your book is priced a lot lower, the reader may think it isn't high quality. If it's priced a lot higher, the reader will think you're trying to price gouge and avoid your book.

Remember, the reader doesn't know how much effort you put into writing the book. They're looking at the finished product and comparing it to other books that look like yours. Color pages, graphics, charts, and images cost more to print but don't register in the reader's mind as increased value at time of purchase.

You'll have to decide if including those features are worth it to the integrity of the book. Five black and white images may be just as good as ten full color images without sacrificing the quality of the content.

When setting the price, take into account your potential profit which is what's left after printing and distribution costs. Your print costs will likely be in the five to six dollar range for each book.

If you sell using one of the online retailers, such as Amazon, they will take a fee for providing the selling platform. Visit Amazon seller central for details.

Don't get discouraged if your profit per book is low. Your book is being used to position you as an authority and generate leads for speaking and other products and services.

Book sales are just one stream of income you will generate from your book and will probably generate the least amount of revenue.

The book is an entry level product in your marketing and sales plan that leads to your higher level products and services.

If you look at your book as lead generation, how many other lead generation tools costing five dollars have the potential to yield thousands of dollars in speaking fees or consulting engagements?

**Expert Author Action: Complete the book cover design**

# CHAPTER 25

## Go to Print

Your manuscript is back from the copy editor, you've purchased an ISBN, you're happy with the cover produced by your book cover designer. It's time to send your manuscript to the printer!

If you're using Scrivener, visit the Literature and Latte website where you purchased Scrivener for complete tutorials on how to compile your manuscript.

After you have a PDF file of your book and book cover, contact a printer to get an estimate of costs and print time. You can use a local printer or one of the online print services. I've used the online printer 48hrbooks.com and have been happy with the quality and service. Their site has a cost calculator which takes you step by step through all of the print options.

You can also use Amazon's publishing service CreateSpace.com. Whether you use a local printer or an online printer, you'll need to make several decisions when getting an estimate on print costs:

- The first option is the binding. I recommend perfect bound. Perfect bound is a paperback book that produces a nice, professional look. The cover has a thicker weight than the pages. Most non-fiction paperback books you see in bookstores are perfect bound. I recommend the standard 60-pound white offset paper and standard 10 point gloss cover.
- The next option is print quantity. I recommend one hundred books or less so you don't end up with a garage or basement full of books you haven't sold. Authors can be too optimistic about the popularity of their books.

I originally printed more than a hundred books for *Maximum Occupancy*, because I had three conferences coming up where I planned to sell my books. I miscalculated the number of attendees who would be interested and didn't sell as many books as I thought.

It took me quite a while to sell the entire inventory. It's true that printing a higher quantity will lower the cost per book but, the print savings disappear if you can't sell them. Start small until you get a feel for the market. You always have the option to print more.

Request a proof copy of the book before placing the final order. A proof copy is one sample copy of the finished book. Some printers include a proof copy at no charge, others will charge a fee. You can request the proof in either pdf or print format.

When working on the timeline for your book launch, build in time to receive and review the proof copy. Allow time to make changes if the proof copy isn't perfect.

If the proof looks good, you will send it to a proofreader for final review.

If you don't like the proof and decide to make changes to your manuscript, you'll need to submit a new pdf file and request a new proof. If you're reviewing multiple PDF proofs, make sure you delete all of the old PDFs so that you don't inadvertently upload an old version.

I can't emphasize enough the need to inspect the proof you receive with a fine-tooth comb regardless of whether you choose print or PDF.

Whatever you approve is what will be printed. If something doesn't look right to you in the proof and it's not something under your control, contact customer service at your printer.

When you're happy with the proof copy, engage a proofreader. As mentioned earlier, your copy editor may also offer proofreader services. If not, follow the same criteria you used when picking an editor to pick a proofreader.

---

**Expert Author Action: Request a proof copy of the book and review for errors and/or required changes.**

---

**Expert Author Action: When you're happy with the proof copy, send to the proofreader.**

---

Expert Author Action: Make any changes recommended by the proof reader. Place the initial quantity order of your book with your printer. I recom-mend one hundred copies or less.

*Linda Griffin*

# Part 4

# Launch Your Book

*"Publishing is a business. Writing may be art,
but publishing, when all is said and done, comes down
to dollars."*

— Nicholas Sparks

*Linda Griffin*

# CHAPTER 26

## Market like a Movie Studio

There are many factors capable of affecting the success of your book. As an expert author, your book will be a source of revenue but revenue from book sales will be much less than the revenue you generate from your other products and services.

Only you can decide what a successful book launch will look like for you. You may find that giving copies of your book away is the best way to generate revenue for your business.

I'm including this section on book marketing because those actions should start well before the book goes to the printer. In fact, marketing should start as soon as you make the commitment to write a book.

The marketing activities I recommend will deliver the biggest impact on a successful book launch.

When you go to see a movie, a series of coming attractions for future movies play prior to the main event. The future movies may not be released until the summer blockbuster season, but studios will start showing the movie trailers in the Winter season.

The movie studios begin building buzz about an upcoming movie well before the release date. Actors will hit the talk show circuit months prior to the movie launch. Sneak peeks behind the scenes will be posted on websites. Video trailers will be shared with fan groups before being released to the general public.

These activities build excitement and anticipation in hopes they will translate to a huge opening weekend at the box office.

On a smaller scale, we want to do the same thing with our books. We want people to be expecting the launch and to be looking forward to anxiously purchasing the book as soon as it's published.

## Start marketing before you start writing

As soon as you've created a book description and working title, announce to your friends and followers your intention to publish a book.

Ask for feedback to start building some buzz. Just like with a movie, if you're comfortable sharing a launch date, include it in your announcement. Otherwise, share the timeframe, such as 'in the Fall' or 'just in time for holiday gift giving'.

## Market while you're writing

As you go through the writing, editing, and publishing process, start setting the groundwork for a successful launch with a book launch marketing plan.

Later on, you will incorporate your book into your overall business marketing plan, but for now, focus on the book launch.

The two components of your book launch marketing plan are:

1. **An Author Platform.** The cornerstone of your book marketing plan is what's called an author

platform. Your author platform is simply all of the ways you use to connect with fans and potential book buyers. The purpose of your author platform is to attract and build a relationship with the people you identify as your ideal readers in order to maximize sales. An author platform consists of a website, social media profiles, and an email list.

2.  A list of marketing actions you will take to generate sales.

# CHAPTER 27

## Author Web Site

An author web site and blog is the home base you'll use to provide access to all of the information about your book in one place. It's what you'll list on your business card and where you'll direct readers to find out about your book along with your other products and services.

Even though you will have a presence on other platforms such as social media, I highly recommend having your own website so that you have total control of your database of fans and followers. The social media platforms change their rules frequently. A change in the rules can result in losing access to the list of buyers and prospective buyers you've worked so hard to develop.

An author website owned and controlled by you:

- ☐ Can be used to sell the book directly or point to the book listing on Amazon.
- ☐ Is where your online media kit will be housed.
- ☐ Will be where you capture names and emails of potential clients who've read your book.

If you have an existing business web site, you can add a new page devoted to your upcoming book. As an alternative, you can create a dedicated author/book website.

With a website and email list, you retain access regardless of what happens on the social media sites.

Fans want to connect with authors. They want to know who they are and experience their personalities.

The best way to do that is to have a website platform where you can showcase your personality and help you sell books and other services.

## Author Media Kit

Create or update your media kit with author and book information. Your media kit should contain:

- A picture of the book cover
- Two head shots of yourself: one holding your book and one without. Black and white and color versions of each.
- Book fact sheet
- Book summary in 150 words
- Book excerpt
- Book reviews
- Book endorsements
- Author info
- Speaking topics
- News angles/interview topics
- Author events calendar
- Media clippings
- Book purchasing info
- Book press release
- Success stories if available

## Examples of Author and book websites

The look and feel of your author website should be consistent with your brand and the book topic. I've included some examples of author websites below to give you some inspiration.

## Guy Kawasaki (guykawasaki.com)

## Book information incorporated into an existing web site

Guy Kawasaki is well-known marketing guru. I heard him speak at a conference a few years ago and was blown away by his personable, down to earth and dynamic presentation.

He has multiple businesses and websites but the one above is his personal site. When you visit the site, notice his choice of images.

The images show Guy interacting with other people one on one or in groups. You're immediately drawn in and feel as if you would like to get to know him.

The site highlights his three focus areas: evangelist, author, and speaker. He's a product evangelist who loves to talk technology and share what he knows.

He's an author who has written 13 books. He's given keynote speeches to people in companies like Apple, Microsoft, and Google as well as smaller ones.

There's a menu item which links to his book page. The book page has images of all the book covers and when you click on them, you're taken to a new page containing a book summary, testimonials, and links to purchase.

## Andrea Q. Robinson. (https://tossthegloss.com/)

### Standalone one page book website

Andrea, who is well known in the fashion industry, wrote a book for women over 50 called *Toss the Gloss*.

Her background includes positions such as chief marketing officer of Estee Lauder, president of Tom Ford Beauty, and president of Ralph Lauren fragrances.

Her book website is a one page site which includes the book cover, book description, price, and ordering information.

Andrea's business site is:

http://www.andreaqrobinson.com/

The web site contains book information as well. Check out both sites to get ideas on how you would like to structure your author website.

## Linda Griffin. (maxoccupancybook.com)

### Standalone book website

For my first book, I chose to create a separate website rather than add a section to my business site. At the time, my business site was for general small business marketing and I didn't have a standalone website for innkeepers.

On the website, I have the book cover and reasons why you would want to buy it. I speak to my ideal reader and tell them what they're going to learn in the book.

I include testimonials from people who've read the book and buttons to buy both the printed copy and the eBook version.

In addition, I include a free download of five promotion ideas from the book. That's a way for web visitors to try the book out before they buy it. It's also a way for me to capture their names and email addresses so I can stay in contact with them.

The site also has a page for the individual chapters. I took the table of contents and reproduced it on the web page.

I include a Resources page containing the resources mentioned in the book. Finally, I have a link to my blog and an events page.

## Alexandra Levit .(alexandralevit.com/)

### Book incorporated into existing website

Alexandra is a workplace consultant who advises companies on how to prepare for the workplace of the future. As expected, the top menu on her site provides a link to her books page.

When you scroll down the home page, you encounter an image and description of one of her bestselling books which also links to her books page. This is a way to capture the attention of someone who may miss the link in the top header.

**Expert Author Action:** Browse the web sites above and look for ideas you can incorporate into your author/book website.

# CHAPTER 28

## Social Media Profiles and Pages

The second component of your author platform is the collection of your social media profiles and pages. You probably already have a business page on Facebook® and a profile on LinkedIn®. You have co-workers and partners who are familiar with your work.

Now you need to make those fans and followers aware of your book project and get them excited about purchasing your book when it comes out. You want them to help spread the word to their circle of connections, and you want to attract new people to your circle.

It will take time to expand your circle which is why I'm recommending you start as soon as you decide to write a book.

Think about your ideal readers and which social platforms they frequent. Those are the platforms on which you should start increasing your activity.

Most of the books we write as business professionals will have some segment of our audience on LinkedIn® so it's a good place to start.

1. Change the headline on your linked in profile. Most people look at the linked in headline as a job title. It will say something like owner of ABC Corporation or Project Manager. When you read the description given by LinkedIn®, It's meant to be a true headline. Instead of owner of ABC Corporation, your headline could say author of the upcoming book and then your book title. It doesn't matter if you don't have your final title. Use the working title. It's easy to change the headline at any time.

2. Add your book project to your LinkedIn® profile. There's a section in your profile to list current projects. Create a project with the title of your book and use your one paragraph book description as the project description. Now anyone visiting your profile will know you're in the

process of writing a book and anyone searching for an expert in your topic will see it in your profile. This is one way you can attract new people and new connections. When you change your profile, your connections get notified so it's an easy way to announce your book.

3. If your ideal readers spend time on Facebook®:

4. Create a Facebook® event for your book launch. It can be a live event or a virtual event depending on how you plan to launch your book. You could even have two events. One that's live for people in your local area and one that's virtual for fans who are remote.

5. Update your Facebook® profile to add author of the upcoming book with the working title.

6. Create a business page as an author. I have a personal profile on Facebook® and a business page called Expertpreneurs which I use to interact with other subject matter experts.

7. If your ideal readers are on Twitter®:

8. Update your Twitter® bio to say author of the upcoming book with the working title. If you want to keep your personal persona separate from your author persona, you could create a

new Twitter® profile of yourself as an author. The only thing you need to create a new Twitter® profile is a different email account.

9.  If your ideal readers are on Pinterest®:

10. Update your Pinterest® bio and create a board for your book topic. Let's say your expertise is in flower arranging. Your book will contain ideas on how to create easy and beautiful flower arrangements from things in your garden. Create an inspiration board containing pictures of arrangements that you like or gardeners that you admire. People who are interested in the topic will search for the topic and discover your board. When you're ready to launch your book, pin a picture of your book cover and link it to Amazon or to the book sales page on your web site.

For both LinkedIn® and Facebook®, join groups related to your topic. Start interacting with the group, asking and answering questions.

When you make a thoughtful answer to a question, people will check your profile and potentially invite you to connect.

# CHAPTER 29

## Email List and Book Reviews

The third component to your author platform is an email list. The primary reason to have your own email list is to increase the probability your fans will see your information.

With the social media platforms, you're dependent upon their rules for how many people will be presented with your posts.

At the time of this writing, the organic reach for Facebook® is around ten percent. That means if you have five hundred fans, only fifty of them are likely to be presented with your post in their news feed.

Email is still the most reliable way to ensure all of your followers will be presented with your information.

I recommend using a professional email marketing service to create and manage your list.

It may be tempting to create a distribution list in your email application and manually send communications. When you do that, you make it harder on yourself to keep the list current.

Email addresses change frequently and readers are sensitive to spam emails. You run the risk of being dropped by your email provider if you receive too many complaints or have too many undeliverable emails.

There are many professional email marketing tools available. If you already have an email marketing tool, simply create a new list for your book audience.

If you don't currently have a professional email marketing tool, I recommend mailchimp.com. It allows you to get started easily and quickly with no cost for the first 2000 subscribers.

Add a sign-up box on your website and provide a sign-up link in email and social media posts.

The benefits of a professional email marketing service are:

1. The deliverability rate is higher. If your list contains valid email addresses, your message will be delivered to one hundred percent of your list.

2. It's in compliance with the CAN-SPAM Act. Subscribers must opt-in to get your information, which makes it less likely they will mark your email as spam. Each email message will have an unsubscribe link or button for people who no longer want to receive communications from you.

3. You get access to reports on who opened the email and who clicked on any links in the email. You can use this information to test subject lines and content to increase the open rates and click through rates.

**What to share with your list**

Start by sending communications to your list in the form of an e-newsletter at minimum on a monthly basis. If you're following the ninety-day schedule, you could increase your communications to every two weeks, instead of monthly. You want to get your followers into the habit of hearing from you as you go through the writing process. Share information with them so when you're ready to launch your book, they're eagerly waiting for it. Your newsletter doesn't have to be long. A one page update of what's happening with your book project is perfect. Anything you share in your newsletter can and should be shared to your social media channels as well in bite sized pieces suitable for the channel.

As you go through the writing and publishing process, share interesting bits of information with your followers. Let's go back to the flower arranging book example from earlier. You're going to be doing some research to determine what types of flower arrangements you want to include. In doing that research, you may find out there are 50 different variations of roses grown in the United States. Share that surprising bit of information in the newsletter.

If you plan to use quotes in your book, periodically share an interesting quote you've decided to use in the final book.

Quotes lend themselves extremely well to Pinterest® and Facebook®. Create a graphic with the quote and pin it to your Pinterest® board or include in your Facebook® status.

There are several online tools you can use to build graphics for Pinterest® and Facebook® easily and quickly. One I recommend is canva.com. The site has pre-made templates sized appropriately for all of the social media platforms. They have stock photos, some free and some for purchase you can use as a base. Then simply type your quote on top of them and publish.

Celebrate all the major milestones leading up to the book launch:

- The planned publish date.
- The book cover creation. You can even have fun with this by sharing more than one version of the cover and asking fans to vote on their favorite.
- When advanced reader copies (ARC) for Beta Readers are available.
- When your book is available for advanced copy purchases.
- Excerpts or sample chapters from the book.
- The book launch party date and details about the event.

Share your writing process, things you've discovered in your research, or how the family is coping with your new project.

Make it personable, giving fans a behind the scenes look at your process. This will get them invested in your success. Always have a call to action in your social media postings and emails. Give the reader an action you want them to take such as:

- Sign up for your mailing list
- Join your Facebook® group
- Follow you on Twitter®
- Connect with you on LinkedIn®
- Recommend your book to someone else
- Buy a second copy of the book as a gift
- Sign up for an eCourse
- Download a free cheat sheet
- Contact you for a speaking engagement
- Sign up for a coaching program
- Hire you for a consulting project

- Register for a live event

## Book reviews

Book reviews are essential to increase sales on Amazon. Book buyers read reviews and use them as a key decision factor when deciding what to purchase.

It's not necessary for every review to be positive. In fact, if all the reviews are five stars, some people get suspicious thinking the reviewers were friends or were paid by the author.

When you send the book to beta readers, you should request they provide an honest review for you on Amazon. Also, as part of your launch activities, ask the purchasers to write a review.

Book Bloggers are another source of book reviews. One way to find them is to search for a book on your topic on Amazon.

Go back to the market research you did when planning your book. Look at the reviewers.

Bloggers and other professional reviewers will have profiles on Amazon. You can reach out to them and offer to send a free copy of your book in exchange for an honest review. Most reviewers will accept the pdf version of the book.

Two blogger directories are bookbloggerlist.com and theindieview.com. Check these directories for people who would be a good fit for your book.

Surprisingly, if you search in Pinterest® for book blogger and click on pinners, you will see book bloggers who have pinned the books they reviewed.

# CHAPTER 30

## Summary

Congratulations! If you've followed the action steps and advice in this book, you have moved from the ranks of those who want to write a book to the elite group of published authors!

You've transformed your knowledge and expertise into something tangible. You've increased your credibility exponentially. You'll be able to set yourself apart from the competition.

Use the book as lead generation for attracting higher paying clients, opportunities for media exposure, and speaking engagements.

Don't forget to claim the templates and checklists I mention throughout the book at

expertauthor411.com/booksmart

As part of the Expert Author family, I invite you to join our Facebook® group for aspiring and published authors.

Join the group at

Facebook.com/groups/ExpertAuthors/

In the group, I provide writing, publishing and marketing tips and inspiration.

# ABOUT THE AUTHOR

After a successful career at a Fortune 500 technology company, Linda Griffin has spent the last ten years working with businesses to increase their credibility and attract customers.

Linda is the author of the book, *Maximum Occupancy: How Smart Innkeepers Put Heads In Beds In Every Season* and is a sought after keynote and workshop presenter.

Linda holds a B.S. in Mathematics from Auburn University and an M.B.A. from the University of South Florida. She resides in Ashburn, Va. with her pets Bugsy the Pug and miniature parrot, Pippin.

To download templates and resources to help you complete your book project, visit her website at expertauthor411.com/booksmart

Connect with Linda on LinkedIn at
linkedin.com/in/LindaGriffin

# Notes